Word Perfe

BOOK SEVEN

BY

RONALD RIDOUT

ILLUSTRATED BY
MARGARET JONES

Ginn and Company Ltd

BOOKS BY THE SAME AUTHOR

Write in English, Books 1-8: a new style of English Workbook providing a carefully graded course on understanding, using and writing English for all 6- to 12-year-olds.

Better English, Introductory Book and Books 1-5: a complete English course from about 6-12 years; illustrated in colour.

English Workbooks, Books 1-8: a graded course in punctuation, spelling, vocabulary, comprehension and composition. The first two are intended for infants.

English Workbooks for the Caribbean, Books 1-8: a workbook course specially written for primary schools in the Caribbean; also suitable for immigrants; illustrated in colour.

Structural English Workbooks, Books 1-8: a carefully graded workbook course teaching English as a foreign language to primary schools in West Africa.

English Now, Books 1-5: a complete course in magazine form for the less academic secondary pupil; illustrated in colour.

© RONALD RIDOUT

Thirteenth impression 1977   157708
ISBN 0 602 20991 9

Published by Ginn and Company Ltd
Elsinore House, Buckingham Street, Aylesbury, Bucks HP20 2NQ

Printed in Great Britain at the University Press, Cambridge

PREFACE

ALTHOUGH the seventh book of *Word Perfect* is still essentially a combined spelling and vocabulary course, its scope has been widened to admit of more discussion of the general history and behaviour of words. Every opportunity has been taken to familiarize the pupil with the story of the growth of our language and to make him realize that it is a living thing that is still growing. For this reason, in addition to examining the various kinds of derivations, I have listed many words to be studied in the living context of idiomatic and figurative expressions.

There is again an increasing emphasis on meaning, so that the Little Dictionary at the end of the book has become a sizable item. It contains all the words whose meaning the pupil is required to elucidate. This ensures a basic training in the use of a dictionary, but the full fruits of this training will be lost unless it is followed up with practice in using a complete dictionary. Work in pronunciation has been taken a stage farther, and this too should be linked with general dictionary training.

Spelling, however, has not been neglected. The basic rules and procedures are constantly referred to, and much of the word manipulation involved in the exercises is aimed at revising the rules and transforming obedience to them into a matter of habit. Most of the pages still carry a word list that the enthusiast for formal spelling can use accordingly ; while every one of the numerous exercises in word-building is a direct aid and incentive to better spelling. At the same time, the book has been so arranged that practically all the spelling work can be accomplished indirectly if the teacher prefers it that way. Indeed, the general guidance and practice in the use of prefixes, suffixes, synonyms, antonyms, homonyms, root words, derivatives, abbreviations, definitions, accent, phonetics, alphabetical order, analogies, etc., would alone justify the time spent on the course, regardless of any desire to improve spelling.

Finally, it should be noted that *Word Perfect*, even in its later stages, is a practical course rather than a purely academic one. It is intended for the general run of pupils rather than for the advanced student. It aims to give the pupil a practical insight into the nature of words that will serve him well in his everyday working and cultural life, and is but little concerned with theory and academic schemata. I therefore set much store by the exercises. It is by practice that most pupils learn best. But it must be correct practice, and I have wherever possible used the self-help method to ensure that it will be correct. The exercises are thus self-teaching rather than self-testing. They are the essential instrument of education in *Word Perfect*.

A set of diagnostic tests have been added to the *Teachers' Manual*, thus providing the teacher with a ready means of gauging the point at which any particular child or group should join the *Word Perfect* course.

HASLEMERE, 1976   R. R.

iii

To the Pupil

To learn to ride a bicycle you practise riding it. When you have ridden it correctly often enough, it becomes a habit: you have learnt to ride it. Yet you probably have very little idea of the theory of balance and dynamics involved.

Much the same thing can happen in learning the meaning and spelling of English words. Provided you practise the word often enough, and practise it correctly, you will in fact learn that word, even if you do not fully understand the theory behind it. If you understand the theory as well, so much the better; but the main thing is to learn the word so that you can use it yourself.

Word Perfect has been based on just this idea. The work has been devised by the self-help method, whereby you can help yourself to do it correctly and so ensure that you do learn it. To make sure that you can ultimately do it correctly, each word of which the meaning is required in the exercises is listed in the Little Dictionary. Whenever in doubt, you should therefore consult this dictionary. Then you will avoid making mistakes and will be learning to your maximum capacity.

It may, however, happen that you do not know the meaning of some of the words you are asked merely to build, and these may not be listed in the Little Dictionary. You should then consult a complete dictionary. In this way you will build up experience in using a vital reference book and need never be at a loss in the world of words when you leave school.

RONALD RIDOUT

see
page
75

This page will help you to make sure of thirty of the words met in earlier books. Join the divided sentences correctly. When in doubt, consult the Little Dictionary on page 75.

Begin like this: 1. "Anxieties" is the plural of the noun anxiety.

1. Anxieties	means to go along with.
2. Finnish	often means clapping.
3. Descent	means the opposite of deliberate.
4. Applause	is the plural of the noun anxiety.
5. Canberra	is the comparative of the adjective stealthy.
6. Hurriedly	means coming from Finland.
7. Comparative	is the capital of Australia.
8. Verifies	is the superlative of the adjective noisy.
9. Accidental	could be applied to an inhabitant of Accra.
10. Annoyance	is the antonym for ascent.
11. Stealthier	means polite behaviour.
12. Ghanaian	is the third person singular of to verify.
13. Superlative	is an adverb formed from to hurry.
14. Antonym	means the highest degree of comparison.
15. Synonym	means the second degree of comparison.
16. Noisiest	means to impose upon or deceive.
17. Maltese	means a word of opposite meaning.
18. Abbreviate	is the adjective formed from Malta.
19. Accompany	wine often comes from Oporto.
20. Portuguese	means to shorten when referring to words.
21. Conceited	means the opposite of serious.
22. Courageous	is the abstract noun from to irrigate.
23. Humorous	means of one's own free will.
24. Mischievous	means having too high an opinion of oneself.
25. Irrigation	means in a reasoned way.
26. Immobile	is a synonym for brave.
27. Voluntarily	means not able to move.
28. Rationally	is synonymous with naughty.
29. Courtesy	means a word of similar meaning.
30. Delude	is a synonym for vexation.

A. Here is another way of revising a great many of the words dealt with in previous books. In each list one word has been wrongly included. State which it is and give your reason for saying so. You may begin like this: 1. "Distinct" is wrongly included because it is an adjective, while all the other words are abstract nouns.

1. friendliness, mystery, distinct, injustice, leisure
2. precious, vicious, delicious, observant, vivacious
3. appearance, admittance, acquaintance, connection
4. generous, expensive, medieval, librarian, obedient
5. Australia, Nigeria, Russia, Dublin, Austria, Egypt

6. patiently, distinctly, obediently, elementary, ably
7. occur, occupy, offend, innocent, illustrate, irritate
8. ankle, shoulder, thigh, knuckle, wrist, cyclist, stomach
9. Eire, Anthony, February, departure, Bedouin, Johnson
10. daughter, laughter, uncle, cousin, ancestor

11. inclusion, cello, invasion, division, laziness, height
12. manageress, duchess, niece, bachelor, spinster
13. collection, congregation, colonel, choir, rabble
14. gnarled, gnome, knowledge, grammar, psalm, knitting
15. measurable, impossible, preferable, comparable

16. autumn, climb, column, summer, solemn, tomb
17. permissible, collapsible, legible, honourable, digestible
18. irregular, incautious, irresponsible, irresolute, irresistible
19. forgotten, extinguished, ate, confessed, chosen, ridden
20. photograph, hyphen, paragraph, coffee, triumph

B. From the words used above, make your own spelling lists of words:

1. ending in –ible   4. beginning with a silent letter
2. beginning with pre–   5. ending with a silent letter
3. ending in –cious   6. ending with –able

despair	economical	appoint	gradually
affection	infinite	authorize	insufficiently
compliment	illustrated	diminish	occasionally
obedience	illegal	relinquish	latterly
disappointment	anxious	relegate	hurriedly

A. For each of the following write down its opposite from the box:

Verbs	Adverbs	Nouns	Adjectives
1. enlarge	6. often	11. hate	16. limited
2. seize	7. formerly	12. hope	17. lawful
3. dismiss	8. suddenly	13. rebellion	18. unworried
4. promote	9. leisurely	14. satisfaction	19. extravagant
5. forbid	10. enough	15. criticism	20. plain

B. Now choose a synonym from the box for each of these:

1. lessen 3. sometimes 5. love 7. limitless
2. recently 4. hastily 6. alarmed 8. hopelessness

C. Fill the blanks with the right words chosen from the box:

1. A — is a form of flattery; it is intended to please.
2. An idea can be — by pictures or by examples.
3. — is the feeling you have towards one you love.
4. If you are not allowed to do it by law, it is —.
5. If something has happened —, it happened in late or recent times.
6. To — a post means to give it up.
7. — is a willingness to do as one is told.
8. When the F.A. — a club, they send it down to a lower division.
9. A committee that gives its secretary the right to do something is said to — him to do it.

In arranging words in alphabetical order, if two or more words begin with the same letter, you must arrange them in order according to their second letters. If their second letters are the same you must arrange them according to their third letters; and so on. Thus *better* comes before *butter*, because *e* comes before *u* in the alphabet. In the same way, *bust* comes before *butter*, because *s* comes before *t*. Then again *better* comes before *betting* because *e* comes before *i*. There is only one other point to remember. If one word has the same letters as another but the other goes on farther, the shorter word always precedes the longer. Thus *ton* comes before *tonsil* and *brother* comes before *brotherly*.

In arranging each of the following lists in alphabetical order you have another opportunity of revising your spelling:

1. butter, better, betting, bust, batter
2. arrange, alphabet, armour, according, abbreviate
3. surgeon, sergeant, courageous, gorgeous, advantageous
4. marvellous, luggage, horrible, application, marrying
5. sandwich, scissors, scenery, separate, satisfactorily
6. pleasant, pheasant, occasion, official, opportunity
7. regretting, rebelling, propeller, marvelled, remodelled
8. preface, precede, previous, preference, presumption
9. wrist, wringer, wrestle, wrapper, written, wreckage
10. unsuitable, unhappily, uncertainty, unsociable
11. denial, desirable, deposited, determination, deliberately
12. inflexible, inaudible, indelible, illegible, intelligible
13. dissimilar, displeasure, disobedience, discourteous
14. suspension, suicide, sufficiently, suffocate, suffice
15. impudence, impressive, impatient, immobile, imperceptible
16. extreme, extremely, explosion, explode, experiment
17. conspicuous, continue, continuation, contemptible
18. irresponsible, irreligious, irresolute, irremovable

In a contemplative fashion
And a tranquil frame of mind,
Free from every kind of passion,
Some solution let us find.
Let us grasp the situation,
Solve the complicated plot—
Quiet, calm deliberation
Disentangles every knot.

(From *The Gondoliers*)

deliberate	passion	disentangle	solve
deliberation	passionate	discriminate	solution
contemplate	dispassionate	discrimination	dissolution
contemplation	variegate	disintegrate	tranquil
contemplative	variegation	disintegration	tranquillizer

A. Find words in the box meaning :
1. to break up or separate into small pieces
2. calm and peaceful
3. something that makes calm and peaceful
4. to see or make a difference between
5. slowness and care in doing or thinking
6. free from emotion or prejudice
7. the fact of being varied in colouring
8. given to looking at or thinking about things for a long time

B. From what verbs ending in –ate do these words come ?
1. contemplative   4. narrative   7. alternately
2. deliberately   5. indicative   8. termination
3. complication   6. advocating   9. abbreviation

C. Before –ate write : gener, invigor, insinu, elev, emigr

D. After dis– write : infect, hearten, embark, close, inter

miraculous	feline	opposite	opposition
populous	supine	appetite	exhibition
poisonous	aquiline	expedite	expedition
anonymous	masculine	exquisite	competition
synonymous	feminine	dynamite	repetition

A. In what way are the two items of each pair alike? Choose your adjective from the box and write sentences like this : 1. They are both supine.

1. a patient on his back and lazy inactive behaviour
2. the nouns *negress* and *vixen*
3. cats and tigers
4. the nouns *drake* and *stallion*
5. a talking mouse and warm ice
6. the adjectives *enormous* and *colossal*
7. London and the Nile Valley
8. arsenic and deadly nightshade
9. a hooked nose and habits like those of an eagle
10. the early ballads and an unsigned letter

B. From what words ending in –ite were these formed?

expedition	exquisitely	ignition	favouritism
opposition	infinity	unity	definition

C. Make nouns ending in –ition from these :

1. definite	4. compete	7. repeat	10. propose
2. expedite	5. compose	8. oppose	11. recognize
3. exhibit	6. impose	9. edit	12. abolish

denial	initial	diary	necessary
burial	partial	salary	elementary
serial	martial	solitary	secondary
material	essential	ordinary	imaginary
cordial	potential	primary	vocabulary

A. Notice that –tial in the second column is pronounced like " shall ". State which of these –tial words means :
1. coming first
2. of the heart; warm and friendly
3. a story published in instalments
4. to do with war
5. capable of coming into being

B. Remember that a word ending in y changes the y into i before adding a suffix. From what words ending in y were these formed ?
1. solitarily　　3. ordinarily　　5. elementarily　　7. denial
2. primarily　　4. imaginarily　　6. secondarily　　8. burial

C. Make adverbs from the following adjectives :
1. essential　　3. serial　　5. ordinary　　7. unnecessary
2. solitary　　4. cordial　　6. necessary　　8. potential

D. Make new words by placing each of these in front of –ary :
1. prim–　　3. can–　　5. second–　　7. gran–
2. di–　　4. milit–　　6. diction–　　8. contr–

E. After ele– write:
gant, ment, mentary, vate, vation, phant

It was abysmally dark. The benighted pedestrian, having reached a cross-road, despaired of taking the correct turning. Eventually he discerned a lofty post, at the top of which there was apparently an inscription. Assuming that this must be a survival of the traditional English signpost meant to be read from the top of a stage-coach, he girded up his loins and began to climb. This arduous task was necessitated by his having only one solitary match left, which he could not risk lighting unavailingly. Near the top he struck his match cautiously and in the ensuing glimmer read: WET PAINT.

caution	nutrition	tradition	describe
cautious	fictitious	traditional	description
sedition	discern	conversation	inscribe
seditious	disciple	conversational	inscription
ambitious	discipline	functional	subscription

A. Ensuing comes from to ensue. From what infinitives do these come?
1. assuming 2. pursuit 3. survival 4. issued 5. arrival

B. From what nouns are these adjectives formed?
1. seditious 3. infectious 5. traditional 7. optional
2. ambitious 4. superstitious 6. exceptional 8. emotional

C. Make an adjective in –al or –ous from each of these:
1. convention 3. flirtation 5. condition 7. nutrition
2. vexation 4. sensation 6. construction 8. proportion

penalty	luxury	estuaries	necessities
penalties	luxuries	tributaries	tyrannies
fatalities	qualities	burglaries	authorities
casualties	celebrities	revolutionaries	commodities
loyalties	peculiarities	specialities	communities

A. Give from the box the word meaning:
1. articles of trade
2. deaths by accident or war
3. persons injured in an accident
4. rivers serving to swell a larger river
5. cruel or unjust acts

B. Remember that nouns ending in y preceded by a consonant change the y into i and add es to form the plural. E.g. anxiety—anxieties; but kidney—kidneys.

Give the singular of these nouns:
1. luxuries   3. peculiarities   5. estuaries   7. impurities
2. penalties   4. commodities   6. diaries   8. enemies

C. Give the plural of these nouns:
1. tributary   3. anxiety   5. quality   7. discovery
2. tyranny   4. dormitory   6. charity   8. opportunity

D. Arrange each of these groups in alphabetical order:
1. novelties, necessities, oddities, opportunities, mutinies
2. royalties, rallies, rarities, remedies, memories
3 chimneys, charities, celebrities, commodities, casualties
4. navies, navvies, nationalities, notified, ninetieth

republic	co-operate	wholesome	independent
justice	co-operative	wholesale	union
athletic	society	amateur	manuscript
athlete	socialism	organization	automobile
television	association	philosophy	authority

A. In writing out the following abbreviations in full you will need at least one of the words in the box for each.

1. I.T.A.   4. A.A.   7. Ph.D.   10. U.N.E.S.C.O.
2. MS.   5. R.A.C.   8. N.U.T.   11. F.R.S.
3. J.P.   6. C.W.S.   9. A.A.A.   12. U.S.S.R.

B. Make words by carrying out these instructions:

1. After manu– write: script, facture, al
2. After auto– write: mobile, graph, matic, biography
3. After co– write: –operative, exist, erce, hort, incide
4. Before –script write: manu, con, post, nonde
5. Before –ile write: mob, sen, juven, gent, fut, infant
6. Before –ity write: author, sincer, secur, minor, ident

C. Give the plural of:

1. charity   3. authority   5. philosophy   7. minority
2. deputy   4. athlete   6. amateur   8. priority

D. Divide these into four classes under the headings:

1. *Containers*   2. *Shopkeepers*   3. *Virtues*   4. *Amusements*

tobacconist	scabbard	satchel	fruiterer
gasometer	florist	barrel	patriotism
integrity	theatre	modesty	draughts
television	milliner	honesty	conjuring

debt	column	almond	foreign
indebted	solemn	becalm	sovereign
debtor	hymn	qualm	feign
subtle	autumn	salmon	campaign
benumb	condemn	alms	gnome

A. What is the silent letter common to all five words in each list in the box?

B. Arrange these words in five equal lists according to the silent letter: g, l, h, b, u.

resign	should	guitar	debtor	guardian
yolk	ghost	subtly	numbed	palm
Thomas	doubtful	signed	honestly	tombstone
plumber	guinea	heiress	calves	rogue
foreigner	rhythm	calmly	feigning	guillotine

C. Place the right word from the box with each definition:

1. to pretend or put on a false appearance of something
2. money or gifts to help the poor
3. owing money or gratitude
4. person who owes something to another
5. to prevent from moving by lack of wind
6. fine, delicate, difficult to appreciate
7. to cause to lose the power of feeling
8. sudden disturbing feeling in the mind

D. Use the Old English prefix be- to derive words from:

1. calm   3. little   5. nighted   7. set   9. spatter
2. numb   4. foul   6. lated   8. muse   10. spectacled

When we speak of the derivation of a word we mean the manner in which it has been formed from another. Some of the words in our language have no apparent derivation; we call them root words. Those formed from the root words are called derivatives. *Night, man, gold, father, garden, bright* are all root words. Derivatives formed from them are: *benighted, manly, golden, fatherly, gardener, brightness.*

Although modern English is founded on Anglo-Saxon or Old English, in the course of centuries numerous French, Latin, Greek and other words have been incorporated into it. Hence our vocabulary today is derived from the words of other languages beside Old English. Some of those foreign words were themselves root words, while others were derivatives. Thus the verb " to move " derives from the root Latin word *movere* (to move), while " motion " derives from *motio*, which is a derivative from *motus* (moved).

Once a word has found its way into the English language, new derivatives are generally formed by adding a particle to the beginning or end of the root word. Particles added to the beginning are called prefixes and most of them were originally English or foreign prepositions like: *with, over, in, ad, circum.* Derivatives formed in this way are usually the same part of speech as the root. Thus *to withstand* comes from *to stand*; *to remove* from *to move*; *overtime* from *time*; *infinite* from *finite*.

Particles added at the end of the root are called suffixes, and derivatives so formed depend for their part of speech mainly on the suffix. Thus from *to move* we have *movable* (adj.), *movingly* (adv.), *movability* (noun); from *to employ* we have *employable* (adj.), *employer* (noun), *employing* (participle).

A. Some prefixes from Old English are: *fore–* (denoting before) as in foretell; *mis–* (wrongly) as in mislead; *a–* (on or in) as in aboard; *out–* (beyond) as in outlive; *over–* (beyond) as in overeat; *un–* (not) as in untrue; *with–* (from or against) as in withstand.

Now pick out the root in these derivatives:

1. unopen   3. forecast   5. aloft   7. outvie
2. overlap   4. overdraft   6. mistake   8. forestall

B. Form words from the following by using an Old English prefix. From each of 10–15 at least two may be formed.

1. haul   4. bode   7. apply   10. state   13. do
2. shore   5. able   8. flank   11. cast   14. board
3. hold   6. fathers   9. asked   12. dress   15. lock

C. Some Old English suffixes used to form nouns are: *–ness, –ship, –dom, –hood, –ing, –er, –ry, –al, –th.* Pick out the root in each of these derivatives, and say whether any change took place in the root as a result of adding the suffix:

1. shyness   4. freedom   7. rivalry   10. strength
2. holiness   5. wisdom   8. removal   11. wedding
3. friendship   6. writer   9. denial   12. livelihood

D. Here are six Latin prefixes and some derivatives formed with their aid. Give the definition of each derivative and make your own spelling lists.

super– (above): supersonic, superfluous, superstructure
bene– (well): benefactor, benevolent, beneficial
ex–, e– (out): expel, expulsion, exclusion, eject, effluent
bi– (twice): bisect, biscuit, biceps, biennial, biped
con– (together): conjunction, conspiracy, confluent, concord
dis– (asunder): disperse, discord, disarray, dispel, disgruntled

incubate	pasture	measure	settlement
incubator	pasturage	measurement	venturesome
duplicator	cleavage	bereavement	grateful
accelerator	storage	announcement	sincerely
accumulator	salvage	endorsement	secretiveness

A. Complete these with the right words from the box:

1. You suffer a — when you lose someone dear to you.
2. Chicks are sometimes hatched in an —.
3. — is the payment made for saving a ship from loss.
4. The way in which a thing tends to split is called its —.
5. A — makes an exact copy of something.
6. We make an — when we write on the back of a document to confirm it.

B. Remember that when we add a suffix beginning with a vowel to a root ending in a silent e, we drop the e. From what root verbs ending in a silent e have these come, then?

1. measurement   3. celebrated   5. indicator   7. investigator
2. pasturage   4. puzzling   6. insulator   8. cultivation

C. Make nouns ending in –or from these root verbs:

1. duplicate   3. narrate   5. conjure   7. collaborate
2. translate   4. navigate   6. contribute   8. interrogate

D. Make a derivative from each of the following by using these suffixes thrice each: –age, –ness, –or, –ment.

1. concise   4. denounce   7. settle   10. reasonable
2. waste   5. deface   8. feeble   11. distribute
3. excavate   6. plume   9. cleave   12. prosecute

creditable	compare	conceivable	justify
preferable	comparable	reconcilable	justifiable
companionable	debatable	inescapable	justifiably
imperturbable	imaginable	indispensable	notifiable
impracticable	excitable	reparable	sociable

A. Define the following adjectives :

1. creditable 2. reparable 3. imperturbable 4. reconcilable

B. Many derivatives have been made with the help of the suffix –able, which came to us from the French language, which borrowed it from Latin. Make adjectives ending in –able from the following root verbs. For the rule about dropping the final e, see p. 14.

1. detach	4. admire	7. value	10. inhabit
2. consume	5. depend	8. excuse	11. analyse
3. consider	6. argue	9. measure	12. repair

C. Now make adjectives ending in –able from these root verbs. For the rule about adding suffixes to words ending in –y, see p. 7.

1. vary	3. envy	5. deny	7. identify
2. notify	4. verify	6. pity	8. punish

D. Notice that to correspond to pronunciation, in adding –ly to words ending in –le, we drop the –le and then add the –ly. Now make adverbs from these adjectives :

1. justifiable	3. variable	5. reasonable	7. indistinguishable
2. preferable	4. sociable	6. deniable	8. incomparable

exempt	extreme	conjecture	constancy
exemption	extremity	conjectural	consumption
exhaustion	excursion	convulsion	concession
extinction	exposure	concentration	conception
expectancy	exasperation	contemporary	conveyance

A. Choose the words from the box having these meanings:
1. belonging to the same time
2. the act of admitting or granting
3. to form an opinion without sufficient proof
4. the state of looking forward to
5. freedom from an obligation

B. Make nouns ending in –ion from these root verbs:
1. exhaust   3. execute   5. consume   7. concede
2. except   4. expedite   6. presume   8. conceive

C. Make nouns ending in –ity from these root adjectives:
1. extreme   2. scarce   3. personal   4. probable

D. Make nouns ending in –ance from these root verbs:
1. convey   2. assist   3. appear   4. ally   5. abound

E. Make derivatives by writing:
1. after con–: viction, verse, trive, temporary, tagious
2. after ex–: cessive, cerpt, clamation, odus, terminate

F. What change in the spelling of the root word has taken place in making these derivatives?
1. scarcity   3. convulsion   5. constancy   7. concession
2. defiance   4. conjectural   6. pleasure   8. presumption

magnetize	heighten	falsify	facilitate
harmonize	coarsen	amplify	infuriate
mobilize	flatten	terrify	gesticulate
devitalize	dishearten	modify	perpetuate
immortalize	chasten	clarify	accentuate

A. Notice that the four endings –ize, –en, –fy, –ate, are all used to make verbs having the force of " to make ". Thus *mobilize* means to make mobile; *coarsen* means to make coarse; *clarify* means to make clear; *infuriate* means to make furious. Now choose the verb that means to make:

1. false
2. clear
3. higher
4. perpetual
5. flat
6. mobile
7. lifeless
8. dejected
9. frightened
10. gestures
11. easy
12. fuller

B. Abstract nouns may be formed from –ize, –ate and –fy verbs like this: mobilize—mobilization; accentuate—accentuation; clarify—clarification. Now form abstract nouns from these verbs:

1. inflate
2. generalize
3. qualify
4. nationalize
5. modify
6. gesticulate
7. unify
8. isolate
9. fraternize
10. pacify
11. mobilize
12. regulate

C. From the following make three derivatives ending in each of these: –ize, –en, –fy, –ate.

1. local
2. quick
3. pure
4. italic
5. sublime
6. valid
7. mad
8. loose
9. simple
10. ample
11. facile
12. dramatic

D. What changes in spelling have the root words undergone in forming the derivatives in Nos. 7–12 of C?

rebutted	billeted	defaulter	dismembered
admitting	bayoneted	interpreter	embroidered
marred	banqueting	depositor	differed
debarred	benefited	balloted	conferred
deferring	patriotic	pivoting	committal

A. Define the following verbs:

1. to rebut   3. to defer   5. to dismember
2. to debar   4. to default   6. to mar

B. Remember that only words accented on the last syllable and ending in a single consonant preceded by a single vowel usually double the final consonant before a suffix beginning with a vowel. Now add –ed to these words that have been divided into syllables and accented for you:

1. lim'-it   3. de-ter'   5. ben'-e-fit   7. diff'-er
2. ad-mit'   4. de-bar'   6. bay'-on-et   8. de-fer'

C. In the same way divide these words into syllables and show the accent. Then add –ing to each.

1. pivot   3. ballot   5. benefit   7. dismember
2. debar   4. banquet   6. deposit   8. interpret

D. Explain why each of these does not double the final consonant of the root word:

1. deserted   3. offering   5. fitment   7. gluttonous
2. cornered   4. fidgety   6. cheated   8. royalist

E. Can you complete these alphabetical lists?

1. –ing: anchoring, baking, cheering, deferring, erring . . .
2. –ful: artful, blissful, cheerful, distrustful . . .

The Latin *venio* (I come) *ventum* (came) is one of the root words from which numerous English words have been derived. Some were already in existence before we started borrowing; others have been built since. The *advent* of a new year means literally its " coming to " us; hence its arrival. An *event* is literally

something that " comes out ", and so it came to signify any occurrence. When an assembly is *convened*, it " comes together ". The noun from this verb, *convention*, thus means " a coming together " of a formal gathering. Similarly, to *contravene* the regulations means to " come against " them or infringe them.

advent	prevent	intervene	refer
revenue	convene	intervention	referred
avenue	convention	contravene	reference
inventor	convenient	conference	transference
eventually	convenience	preference	deference

A. The first thirteen words derive from *venio*. Work out their original meanings and give them alongside their actual meaning.

B. Do likewise with the last seven which all derive from *fero* (I bring).

C. Notice that it is *conferred* but *conference*. In the latter the final r of con-fer' is not doubled because in adding the suffix the accent is shifted to the first syllable (con'-fer-ence). Now make nouns in −ence from these verbs :

1. refer   2. prefer   3. defer   4. differ   5. transfer

to be afflicted with	to acquit of
to be addicted to	to acquiesce in
to succumb to	to impose upon
to accede to	to be adjacent to
to disapprove of	to be inferior to
to be aggravated by	to be covetous of
to be exempt from	to be guiltless of
to persevere in	to be different from
to sympathize with	to be indifferent to

You will observe from the above list that certain words are followed by particular prepositions. A few, however, change the preposition according to usage. Thus we say indignant with someone, but indignant at a happening; correspond with someone (i.e. exchange letters), but correspond to the facts (i.e. agree with); to divide among many, but to divide between two.

A. Define the following words:

1. to succumb   3. to aggravate   5. to exempt   7. adjacent
2. to accede   4. to acquiesce   6. to acquit   8. covetous

B. Complete these with the right words from the top list:

1. He lived to see two more monarchs — to the throne.
2. His fever was — by lying in a draught.
3. He earned so little that he was — from income tax.
4. I was sorry to see him — to temptation and steal the money but I could not — in this dishonest behaviour.
5. Afterwards he was — with a sense of guilt.
6. The jury could not — him of the charge of theft since he was not — of it, but they did — with his remorse.

C. Write sentences to bring out the meaning of:

1. different from   3. to persevere in   5. adjacent to
2. correspond to   4. addicted to   6. covetous of

A. Solve this puzzle. Check with the Little Dictionary.

Across

5. Pipe player
8. Emotions
9. Sloop for fishing
10. Opposite of exterior
11. Rascal
14. Half a score
16. A British Dominion near U.S.A.
17. A thing's existence as opposed to its qualities
18. At this moment
20. Synonym for swoon
24. Exact and precise
25. Taxes paid for use of road, etc.
26. Shaped like a circle (adj.)
27. Full of wit

Down

1. To fix or fasten to or on
2. Noteworthy acts of valour
3. Substance such as flax
4. Antonym for to notice
6. Freedom from disease, etc.
7. Dig out, leaving a hole
12. Long tubes of wheaten paste
13. Stout glove with long wrist
14. The bronze of sunburnt skin
15. Fresh
19. Flower ending with "hid"
21. The people of Holland
22. Cataracts
23. Drops from the eye

B. Complete this puzzle in any way you like, and then draw up suitable clues for it.

Give one word for each of the following:

1. calm and peaceful   (page 5)
2. death by accident or war   (9)
3. court card; rascal   (21)
4. a story published in instalments   (7)
5. a word of opposite meaning   (1)
6. to make undying; to confer undying fame upon   (17)
7. a river serving to swell a larger river   (9)
8. the opposite of formerly   (3)
9. having a hooked nose; like an eagle   (6)
10. to make friends with   (17)
11. the capital of Australia   (1)
12. capable of coming into being   (7)
13. words written on monument, coin, etc.   (8)
14. person who owes something to another   (11)
15. to make partial changes in   (17)
16. freedom from punishment, disease, etc.   (21)
17. desirous of doing good; well-wishing   (13)
18. the opposite of a professional   (10)
19. to come between so as to affect the result   (19)
20. able to be collapsed   (2)
21. book or document written by hand   (10)
22. of unknown name   (6)
23. courteous submission, especially to one's superiors   (19)
24. to go before   (4)
25. directed against the authority of the state   (8)
26. free from emotion or prejudice   (5)
27. having the same meaning   (6)
28. a sudden disturbing feeling in the mind   (11)
29. not able to be thrown into confusion   (15)
30. lying face upward   (6)
31. the writing on the back of a document to confirm it   (14)
32. to see or make a difference between   (5)

First Spelling Test

(1)

attention	alligator	confidential	profitable
accordion	radiator	substantial	acceptable
appetite	debtor	essential	regrettable
annoyance	accelerator	impartial	invaluably
supplement	territory	potentially	invariably

(2)

secretaries	wholesome	committee	occurring
hostilities	subtly	wholly	preferred
societies	campaign	pyjamas	deterrent
necessities	handkerchief	icicle	dismissal
anxieties	succumb	moustache	admittance

(3)

doubly	prosecution	exterminate	approval
proposal	excavation	facilitate	announcement
imaginative	insulation	horrify	accomplishment
ventilation	accumulation	emphasize	disappointment
ignorance	collaboration	materialize	suicidal

Dictation

Probably none of our contemporaries could immediately give the correct spelling of every word in our language. We should not, however, think that as a consequence there is no necessity to improve our own spelling. Complacency is merely a cover for funk. It is considerably more grown-up to be conscious of our deficiencies and seek to remedy them. For if we are sufficiently determined, and if we practise patiently with convenient material, improvement will undoubtedly come.

spectator	science	baptize	pacifist
refrigerator	audience	baptism	pacifism
dormitory	experience	hypnotize	communist
laboratory	lenience	hypnotism	communism
directory	resilience	journalism	feudalism

A. By referring to the Little Dictionary, write definitions of:

1. baptism 3. feudalism 5. journalism 7. pacifism
2. directory 4. hypnotize 6. lenience 8. resilience

B. Complete each of these analogies with a word from the box:

1. National is to nationalism as feudal is to —.
2. — is to subject as iron is to metal.
3. Theatre is to plays as — is to experiments.
4. Sleeping is to — as cooking is to kitchen.
5. Oven is to heat as — is to cold.
6. — is to addresses as index is to subject-matter.
7. Poet is to verse as reporter is to —.
8. Gentle is to — as harsh is to strictness.
9. — is to elasticity as immensity is to hugeness.
10. Oil is to anoint as water is to —.
11. — is to war as vegetarian is to meat.
12. Inexperience is to — as disagreement is to agreement.
13. Players is to team as listeners is to —.
14. — is to public ownership as royalist is to monarchy.
15. Look is to — as speak is to orator.
16. Execute is to death as — is to trance.

C. Try to complete this alphabetical series:
    actor, bisector, concoctor, director, educator . . .

refugee	ammunition	sergeant	camouflage
volunteer	garrison	colonel	manœuvre
recruit	strategy	subaltern	guerrilla
infantry	armistice	adjutant	reconnoitre
armour	disarmament	lieutenant	reconnaissance

What is each of the following called? The answers are in the box. Begin like this: 1. An officer next below a captain is called a lieutenant.

1. an officer next below a captain
2. civilians who enter military service of their own free will
3. the science of directing great military operations
4. any commissioned officer below the rank of captain
5. the examination of a tract of country
6. a newly enlisted soldier
7. foot soldiers
8. troops, often civilians, who carry on war behind the lines
9. the reduction of military forces
10. temporary stop in fighting, by agreement
11. protective covering
12. soldiers stationed in a town to defend it
13. bullets, shells, powder for weapons
14. the officer commanding a regiment
15. the officer who assists a commanding officer
16. non-commissioned officer ranking above a corporal
17. to make a survey of the enemy's position and strength
18. a planned movement of troops
19. the disguise of objects to deceive the enemy
20. anyone who flees for safety

aches = aykz

aisle = yl

ampersand = am'-per-sand

aria = ah'-ri-a

ascetic = as-set'-ic

boatswain = bohz'-un

buffet (sideboard) = boo'-fay

buffet (knock) = buf'-it

centenary = sen-teen'-a-ree

chaperon = shap'-er-ohn

circuitous = ser-kew'-it-us

comparable = kom'-par-a-bl

controversy = kon'-tro-ver-see
       or kon-trov'-er-see

czar = zah

dais = days

disreputable = dis-rep'-ew-ta-bl

envelop = en-vel'-op

envelope = en'-ve-lohp

escort (verb) = es-kort'

escort (noun) = es'-kort

espionage = es'-pee-on-ij

forfeit = for'fit

indicative = in-dik'-a-tiv

infinite = in'-fin-nit

infinitive = in-fin'-i-tiv

invalid (sick) = in'-va-leed

invalid (void) = in-val'-id

lieutenant = lef-ten'-ant

parenthesis = pa-ren'-thi-sis

polygamy = po-lig'-a-mee

poste restante = pohst-res-tahnt'

reparable = rep'-ar-a-bl

viscount = vy'-kownt

To help you pronounce the above words correctly, they have been divided into syllables, the accented syllable shown by a stroke and their pronunciation indicated by a simple phonetic system. In this system the soft hissing consonant is represented by s, the hard hissing one by z, and the hard c sound by k. The vowel sounds are represented by these letters:

a as in late = ay

a as in father = ah

a as in cat = a

e as in feet = ee

e as in pet = e

i as in fight = y

i as in hit = i

o as in no = oh

o as in not = o

u as in tune = ew

u as in rule = oo

u as in but = u

ou as in bout = ow

PAGE TWENTY-SEVEN (27)

A. With the help of the Little Dictionary, choose the word on the opposite page that means:

1. not respectable in character or appearance
2. not valid; having no legal force
3. to wrap up or surround
4. raised platform, especially for seat like a throne
5. able to be compared; similar
6. argument on a subject about which different opinions exist
7. refraining from pleasures and comforts
8. the sign (&) that means *and*
9. the practice of having more than one wife at a time
10. roundabout; not direct
11. a melody for a single voice, especially in opera
12. a married or elderly woman in charge of girl on social occasion

B. Divide each of these words into three syllables, and show the accent and pronunciation by the same system as used on the opposite page. Then check your answers with the list.

1. envelope   3. chaperon   5. invalid (sick)   7. aria
2. ampersand   4. infinite   6. ascetic   8. envelop

C. Treat these words of four syllables in the same way:

1. centenary   3. infinitive   5. espionage
2. polygamy   4. indicative   6. parenthesis

D. The following words will not be found in the list. Try to deal with them in the same way. There are four words of two syllables, five of three syllables and three of four syllables.

1. mauve   4. pursue   7. infinitely   10. escorted
2. orgy   5. queue   8. stomach   11. panorama
3. psalm   6. scissors 9. spinach   12. parenthetical

The table below provides examples of words derived from certain Latin root nouns. The Latin word *via*, meaning the way, is a good illustration of how these derivatives are formed. An *obvious* thing is something that stands in the way and cannot be avoided. To *obviate* means to meet in the way and, hence, to prevent. *Devious* meant literally from the way, and so came to mean going out of the way. Thus if you *deviate* you go out of the normal way. Finally, *impervious* has the literal meaning of not through the way or, in other words, not penetrable.

1. *via* (way): obvious, obviate, devious, deviate, impervious
2. *signum* (sign): signify, insignificant, assign, insignia
3. *manus* (hand): manual, manicure, manacle, manufacture
4. *poena* (pain): punish, penal, penitence, repent
5. *litera* (letter): literature, illiterate, literal
6. *annus* (year): annual, per annum, anniversary, annuity

A. Write out the table and add two more examples to each line from the following list:

ensign	manipulate	previous	convoy
superannuate	perennial	penalty	impunity
manuscript	obliterate	literary	countersign

B. Define the following: 1. impunity 2. annuity 3. assign 4. insignia 5. penitence 6. manacle.

C. Try to show how these words were derived:
1. previous 2. manuscript 3. illiterate 4. superannuate

Westmorland	Derbyshire	Berkshire
Cornwall	Durham	Shropshire
Cambridgeshire	Gloucestershire	Somerset
Glamorganshire	Surrey	Warwickshire
Cumberland	Lancashire	Hampshire
Essex	Leicestershire	Worcestershire
Denbighshire	East Sussex	

A. Write out the counties and number them down the lists
1–20. Then after each one write the county town. If you do
this correctly, the towns will be in alphabetical order.

Kingston-upon-Thames	Shrewsbury	Leicester	Lancaster
Chelmsford	Gloucester	Worcester	Winchester
Cardiff	Cambridge	Durham	Lewes
Carlisle	Derby	Appleby	Reading
Taunton	Warwick	Bodmin	Denbigh

B. Group these in six equal classes of rivers, mountains,
counties, cities, continents and oceans:

Shropshire	Asia	Ibadan	Australasia
Everest	Thames	Africa	Mississippi
Europe	Shanghai	Yangtse	Antarctic
Missouri	Arctic	Atlantic	Edinburgh
Middlesex	Pacific	Bucharest	Urals
Pyrenees	Ayrshire	Apennines	Roxburgh

C. The county name of Suffolk is derived from South Folk,
while Middlesex was once known as the land of the Middle
Saxons. Now try to find out the derivation of these names:

1. Essex   2. Norfolk   3. Sussex   4. East Anglia

bier	crevasse	enterprise	accurate
soldier	bassoon	chastise	accustom
bombardier	harass	compromise	accountant
cavalier	mannequin	improvise	accumulate
premier	corrugate	merchandise	accomplish

A. From the box find the noun naming a person who:

1. earns a living by wearing and showing off clothes
2. is an artillery non-commissioned officer below a sergeant
3. inspects accounts professionally
4. was a horseman, especially in the seventeenth century
5. is the Prime Minister of G.B. or some British dominions

B. Now find a verb meaning to:

1. say or do something without preparation
2. vex or worry by repeated attacks
3. contract into ridges, wrinkles or folds
4. to settle by a partial yielding on both sides
5. beat or punish

C. Complete these sentences with words from the box:

1. A coffin is usually taken to the grave on a —.
2. A — is a wooden double-reed instrument used as bass to the oboe.
3. The opposite of to — is to disperse or scatter.
4. A deep split in the ice of a glacier is called a —.

D. How much of each series can you complete?

1. amplifier, brigadier, cashier, defier, envier . . .
2. accomplishment, banishment, chastisement, derailment . . .

original	expand	wouldn't	feudal
farcical	expansion	you're	corporal
prodigal	comprehension	they'll	equality
principal	extension	it's	pretentious
cathedral	suspension	won't	o'clock

A. Give the word meaning :

1. spending to excess or without necessity
2. to do with the body (adj.)
3. first or most important
4. appropriate to farce ; ludicrous
5. doing things for show or to cut a fine figure (adj.)

B. Notice that words like expand drop the d when adding –sion. Now form nouns ending in –sion from these verbs :

1. extend   2. suspend   3. comprehend   4. pretend

C. Make a word ending in –al from each of these :

   1. origin   3. refuse   5. bury   7. person
   2. deny   4. arrive   6. crime   8. idea

D. Make a noun ending in –ity from each of these :

   1. equal   3. scarce   5. stupid   7. secure
   2. original   4. odd   6. timid   8. absurd

E. Write the abbreviation from the box that stands for :

   1. it is   3. will not   5. of the clock
   2. you are   4. they will   6. would not

F. Make adverbs ending in –ly from these adjectives :

1. principal   3. extensive   5. equal   7. comprehensive
2. original   4. criminal   6. essential   8. decisive

Food	Animals	Crime	Education
cucumber	buffalo	offence	academic
cauliflower	giraffe	accomplice	syllabus
lettuce	gorilla	assailant	professor
onion	hyena	assassination	technical
rhubarb	leopard	conspiracy	grammar
celery	reindeer	embezzlement	composition
biscuits	rhinoceros	larceny	mathematics
marmalade	dachshund	delinquent	wrangler
sandwiches	retriever	suicide	theoretical
sausages	hippopotamus	acquittal	curriculum

A. Arrange each list in alphabetical order.

B. Find the words in the lists meaning :

1. a theft
2. an attacker
3. offending
4. scholarly
5. a person aiding another in crime
6. a setting free by declaring not guilty
7. a theft of money entrusted to one's care
8. a complete set of courses for study

C. Prepare the following paragraph for dictation :

Has it ever occurred to you to associate spelling-bees with the early nineteenth century? That was their period of greatest popularity. Their revival in the epoch of television is intelligible enough. We all like acquiring knowledge in as pleasant a manner as possible, and spelling-bees combine practical instruction with the opportunity for social amusement. The very fact that we enjoy the occasion ensures our undivided attention. Spelling-bees possess another distinct advantage : the Question Master or Master of Ceremonies, as he is sometimes designated, will pronounce the words carefully, and correct pronunciation is essential for good spelling.

retailer	optimist	musician	athlete
poulterer	pessimist	optician	delegate
loiterer	specialist	politician	magistrate
collier	capitalist	electrician	bursar
grazier	socialist	physician	scholar

A. Write these sentences, inserting the right words from the box :

1. A — fattens cattle for the market.
2. He asked the — to sell him a pair of spectacles.
3. The treasurer of a college is usually called the —.
4. Unlike the wholesaler, the — sells direct to the consumer.
5. The — puts the most cheerful interpretation to the facts, whilst the — puts the gloomiest.
6. — is the name given to a coal-miner, but it also means a ship carrying coal.
7. A — is an elected representative sent to a conference.
8. Criminal cases are tried in the police court by a — who is sometimes known as a Justice of the Peace.

B. Form nouns ending in –ist from the following :

1. capital 3. flute 5. cycle 7. alarm
2. type 4. violin 6. tour 8. piano

C. Some nouns ending in –ist give rise to adjectives ending in –ic. Form adjectives by adding –ic to these nouns :

1. optimist 3. realist 5. militarist 7. modernist
2. pessimist 4. artist 6. socialist 8. atheist

D. Continue these series :

1. avenger, beholder, commander, dawdler . . .
2. atheist, banjoist, cyclist, dramatist, egotist . . .

trivial	crucial	temporary	constable
genial	artificial	stationary	constabulary
menial	financial	voluntary	insanitary
ceremonial	provincial	secretarial	itinerary
proverbially	commercial	necessarily	involuntarily

A. Use the right word from the box to fill each blank:

1. A — car is one that is standing still.
2. If you do something —, you are not acting of your own free will.
3. A — companion is someone whom you find cheerful and friendly.
4. — tasks were those done by a servant rather than his master.
5. A — decision is one on which much depends.
6. The route taken on a long journey is often called the —.

B. Use the following words in similar sentences of your own:

1. trivial   2. ceremonial   3. temporary   4. insanitary

C. Make adverbs from the following adjectives:

1. genial   3. artificial   5. voluntary   7. unofficial
2. cordial   4. commercial   6. temporary   8. unnecessary

D. Make adjectives in –ary from these words:

1. custom   3. prime   5. revolution   7. imagine
2. moment   4. second   6. supplement   8. discipline

E. Derive at least one word from each of these:

1. secretary   3. ceremony   5. voluntary   7. tribute
2. province   4. constable   6. finance   8. crux

Messenger of sympathy and love,
Servant of parted friends,
Consoler of the lonely,
Bond of scattered family,
Carrier of news and knowledge,
Instrument of trade and industry,
Promoter of mutual kindness,
Of peace and goodwill
Among men and nations.

(*Inscription on Post Office at Washington, U.S.A.*)

console	fibre	sympathy	industry
consolation	metre	sympathetic	industrial
promote	meagre	apathy	mutual
promotion	goitre	apathetic	intellectual
locomotion	calibre	telepathy	metric

A. Complete these sentences with words from the box:

1. The — of a gun barrel is often expressed in centimetres.
2. To be — about the — system means to be indifferent about a measuring system based on the decimal.
3. If X and Y show — affection, X likes Y in the same way as Y likes X.

B. From what nouns are these adjectives derived?

1. apathetic   2. telepathic   3. metric   4. industrial

C. From what root words are these derived? What change has the root undergone in Nos. 4–8?

1. individuality   3. punctuality   5. promotion   7. carrier
2. eventuality   4. devotion   6. consoler   8. quotation

PAGE THIRTY-SIX (36)

A. Pronounce carefully:

(*a*) the sound of o as in bone (international phonetic symbol ou)
(*b*) the sound of o as in stop (phonetic symbol ɔ)
(*c*) the sound of o as in one (phonetic symbol ʌ)
(*d*) the sound of o as in tomb (phonetic symbol u :)
(*e*) the sound of or as in cord (phonetic symbol ɔ :)

Then find from the box below six words containing each sound. Write them in five lists—(*a*), (*b*), etc.

trophy	formula	stomach	cosmetics	adorable
compass	college	soldier	profile	motif
losing	support	proving	combination	onions
rotary	approve	drawer	loveliness	womb
boarder	comma	honey	canoeing	cousin
contract	copied	protract	ordinarily	lasso

B. Complete each sentence below with one of these italicized words containing the root "tract" from *tracto* (I draw), *tractus* (drawn):

subtraction *tractable* *protracted* *abstract* *attracted*
extracting *detract* *distracted* *retract* *tractors*

1. Any steel object is — by a magnet.
2. Do you find — more difficult than addition?
3. An — noun names a quality drawn from things.
4. Ploughs in England are now usually pulled by —.
5. The dentist had difficulty in — the tooth.
6. The meeting was a — one, lasting many hours.
7. What you said was quite wrong, and you had better — it.
8. His attention was — by the noise of the jet aircraft.
9. Nothing that you say will — from his popularity.
10. A — child can be easily led or handled.

destroy	legible	eligible
destruction	illegible	ineligible
destructible	irresistible	exhaustion
indestructible	perceive	inexhaustible
incorruptible	perception	inexpressible
combustion	perceptible	incomprehensible
combustible	imperceptible	indivisible

A. Use the right words from the box to complete these:
1. Something that is — cannot be destroyed.
2. Anything capable of burning is said to be —.
3. — writing cannot be read.
4. An — difference is so small that it cannot be perceived.
5. If a person is not able to be elected, we say he is —.

B. Give the abstract noun ending in –ion corresponding to:
1. destructible   4. comprehensible   7. expressible
2. indigestible   5. exhaustible   8. convertible
3. combustible   6. corruptible   9. divisible

C. From what verbs were these adjectives formed?
1. digestible   3. reversible   5. discernible   7. defensible
2. suppressible   4. perceptible   6. convertible   8. admissible

D. Make adjectives ending in –ible from these verbs:
1. collapse   3. perceive   5. permit   7. divide
2. comprehend   4. destroy   6. sense   8. perfect

E. The prefix in- is used to express the opposite. Before b
and p it becomes im–. Before l it becomes il, and before r it
becomes ir–. Now make opposites of these:
1. credible   3. possible   5. legible   7. audible
2. divisible   4. permissible   6. resistible   8. eligible

The Latin for I sit is *sedeo*, **and** the past participle is *sessum*. There are numerous derivatives from this in English. To *preside* over a meeting means literally to sit before others, and so in authority over them. The person who sits in authority is thus the *president*. In the same way to *supersede* someone means to sit above him and hence displace him. The Latin word appears again in *residence*, the place where one normally sits or stays. Then the *residue* is that part which sits or remains after some has been removed. The Latin root appears again in *subside*, *dissident*, *sediment*, *sedentary*, *assiduous* and *sedulous*. When a flood *subsides*, it sits under, that is settles down. A *dissident* member is one who sits apart from the rest and hence disagrees. *Sediment* is that which sits or settles at the bottom of a liquid. A *sedentary* occupation is one requiring much sitting. An *assiduous* worker is one who is always sitting at his work and is therefore diligent. Finally, to attend to one's work *sedulously* is to do it with diligence.

residence	subsidy	sedate	supersede
residue	subsidize	sediment	insidious
preside	subsidiary	sedentary	assiduous
subside	settle	sedulous	dissident
subsidence	session	sedative	presidency

Write definitions of these words:

1. insidious
2. residue
3. to preside
4. to supersede
5. to subside
6. dissident
7. sedentary
8. assiduous

delicious	audacious	luscious	contagion
spacious	audacity	vicious	contagious
malicious	capacious	suspicion	religious
conscious	capacity	suspicious	prodigy
consciousness	ferocious	graciously	prodigious

A. Place the right word from the box with each definition:

1. spread by contact (adj.)
2. richly sweet in taste or smell; very delicious
3. a marvellous thing, especially one out of the course of nature
4. the quality of being aware or of knowing
5. showing active ill-will; having vindictive feelings

B. Notice that the rule on page 14, about adding a suffix beginning with a vowel, is broken by words ending in –ce or –ge (courage—courageous). This is so that the c or g may be kept soft. Sometimes, however, the e is turned into an i, which has the same effect (grace—gracious). Now form adjectives from these nouns:

1. outrage
2. advantage
3. space
4. grace
5. malice
6. vice
7. avarice
8. caprice

C. To what adjectives do these nouns correspond?

1. spaciousness
2. preciousness
3. ferocity
4. capacity
5. contagion
6. suspicion
7. atrocity
8. fallacy

D. Make two equal lists of the following according to whether they name moving water or still water: lake, lagoon, torrent, brook, cascade, rivulet, pond, cataract, pool, jet, reservoir, puddle.

disguise	dissatisfaction	misgovern	mischievous
disqualify	dissent	misapply	misguided
distribution	dissension	miscalculate	misbehaviour
disappearance	dissuade	misinterpret	mis-statement
disapproval	dissolution	misjudgment	mis-shapen

Notice that the prefix mis– usually suggests " amiss " or " wrongly "; while dis– suggests " away from " or simply the opposite of the root word.

Remember that a double s occurs only when the root word to which the prefix dis– or mis– is added begins with an s.

A. Now make new verbs by adding dis– to these:

1. satisfy   3. approve   5. prove   7. respect
2. appear   4. qualify   6. possess   8. organize

B. Make new nouns by adding mis– to these:

1. behaviour   3. calculation   5. government   7. guidance
2. conception   4. interpretation   6. judgment   8. spelling

C. Make these adjectives into their opposites by using dis–:

1. satisfied   3. similar   5. respectful   7. inclined
2. qualified   4. courteous   6. obedient   8. passionate

D. Use mis– to make these verbs name wrong actions:

1. behave   3. spell   5. pronounce   7. manage
2. govern   4. state   6. represent   8. interpret

E. Define:

1. mis-shapen   2. dissuade   3. dissent   4. dissolution

F. Which word in the box breaks the rule about dropping a final e?

opportunity	literary	catalogue	technique
appreciation	literacy	dialogue	physique
illusion	vocabulary	monologue	antique
illustrated	complimentary	epilogue	antiquity
intelligible	proprietary	intrigue	iniquity

A. Complete the sentences below by using these phrases:

literary criticism	unbounded opportunity
standard of literacy	proprietary brands
illustrated catalogue	vocabulary building
new techniques	complimentary ticket
lively dialogue	warm appreciation

1. He showed his — of my efforts by raising my wages.
2. — is one of the main aims of *Word Perfect*.
3. The art of evaluating literature is called —.
4. The — of a country depends upon how well its people are taught to read and write.
5. The — contained pictures of the goods offered for sale.
6. There need be no frustration in a country of —.
7. — is an essential ingredient of a good play.
8. Modern engineering firms utilize many — of construction.
9. — are those articles clearly bearing the trade mark of the manufacturers.
10. A — at first sight sounds as if it bears flattering words, and in a sense it does, since it is received as a gift, and gifts are a form of flattery.

B. Define:

1. monologue   2. epilogue   3. antiquity   4. iniquity

retort	concluded	amplified	assurance
refute	responded	notified	rejoinder
recant	acknowledged	certified	accusal
resume	allude	verified	observation
resumption	allusion	verification	assumption

A. Fill the blanks with the right words from the box:

1. If the statement has been —, the details have been filled in.
2. If it has received —, its truth has been established.
3. When you — you take back all you have said.
4. He will — the accusal by showing it to be utterly unfounded.
5. A —, like a —, is anything said in reply.

B. Make new words by carrying out these instructions:

1. After re– write: fute, frain, sume, sponse, cant, ject, joice.
2. After con– write: firm, clude, fess, fute, form, front, demn.
3. Before –fied write: noti, justi, mysti, magni, glori, clari.

C. Can you complete this table?

	Verb	Noun	Adjective	Adverb
1.	to observe	—	observant	—
2.	—	co-operation	—	co-operatively
3.	to conclude	—	—	conclusively
4.	—	presumption	presumptive	—
5.	to assure	—	assured	—
6.	—	justification	—	justifiably
7.	to allude	—	—	allusively
8.	—	suspicion	—	suspiciously
9.	—	apology	apologetic	—
10.	to persuade	—	—	persuasively

similar	curiosity	acquaintance	monster
particular	verbosity	countenance	monstrous
jocular	pomposity	exuberance	disaster
triangular	monstrosity	remembrance	disastrous
rectangular	animosity	encumbrance	ludicrous

A. With the help of the clues and the Little Dictionary, give the words asked for below. They are not all in the box.

1. shaped like a circle (cir—)
2. to do with the North and South Poles (po—)
3. having the shape of a tube (tub—)
4. having the shape of a triangle (tri—)
5. concerning the stars (ste—)
6. to do with the sun (so—)
7. to do with the moon (lu—)
8. given to joking (j—)
9. standing up at right angles to the base (per—)
10. making a great display (spec—)

B. You will improve your speech and spelling by practising the following and preparing them for dictation:

1. Similarly, this particular scholar was not unpopular as the result of his jocular use of a peculiar collar.
2. The advertisement concluded with an unintelligible allusion to Disraeli's assertion that Gladstone was inebriated with the exuberance of his own verbosity.
3. Curiously, he presumed to believe that the acquisition of numerous acquaintances among judges would achieve his acquittal. This monstrous assumption would have been ludicrous if it had not been so disastrous.

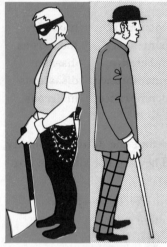

To *galvanize* derives from the name of Galvani the Italian scientist, while *ohm* derives from the name of a German physicist who died in 1854. But even if we exclude scientific and technical terms, there are considerable numbers of words in the English language which are derived from personal names. Two particularly interesting ones are *derrick* and *bowler*. The word *derrick*, which means a kind of crane or hoisting apparatus, derives from the name of a notorious executioner in Elizabethan times. A certain Mr Bowler gave his name to the bowler hat in more recent times, for it was on 8th August 1868 that he announced in the *Daily News* that he had invented and was selling " a new hat that is completely ventilated, whilst at the same time the head is relieved of the pressure experienced in wearing hats of the ordinary description ".

notorious	pensioner	physics	dahlia
notoriety	executioner	physicist	boycott
pious	questioner	technical	derrick
piety	confectioner	technician	apparatus
anxious	commissioner	mathematician	ventilator

By consulting a good dictionary try to find out from what personal names these words were derived :

1. dahlia 2. burke 3. ampère 4. wellingtons 5. boycott

1. lasting or meant only for a time   (page 34)
2. spending extravagantly   (31)
3. the officer who assists a commanding officer   (25)
4. a farmer who fattens cattle for the market   (33)
5. the sign meaning *and*   (27)
6. the act of settling down or sinking in level   (38)
7. exemption from punishment   (28)
8. person tending to look at the gloomiest aspect of things   (33)

9. the raised platform on which a throne might rest   (27)
10. able to be repaired   (15)
11. to take back what you have said   (42)
12. person aiding another in crime   (32)
13. involving much sitting   (38)
14. not able to be resisted   (37)
15. showing active ill-will (adj.)   (39)
16. a disguise to protect something from observation   (25)

17. indifferent, showing no enthusiasm   (35)
18. not able to be understood   (37)
19. a deep split in the ice of a glacier   (30)
20. the quality of being gentle and undisposed to severity   (24)
21. the state of being sorry or repentant   (28)
22. docile; easily handled or managed   (36)
23. to compose, speak or entertain without preparation   (30)
24. the spread of disease by contact   (39)

25. the quality of being devout or religious   (44)
26. to make gestures   (17)
27. to settle by a partial yielding on both sides   (30)
28. to disprove or force back a statement, charge, etc.   (18)
29. contrivance for hoisting heavy weights   (44)
30. belonging to the same time   (16)
31. the act of establishing the truth of something   (42)
32. appropriate to a servant   (34)

Second Spelling Test

(1)

parasite	interference	affection	renegade
satellite	circumference	appreciation	language
idolize	indifference	exaggeration	centigrade
aquiline	coincidence	application	thoroughfare
homicide	correspondence	opposition	associate

(2)

customary	voluminous	allotment	league
extraordinary	treacherous	allusion	intrigue
honorary	iniquitous	allege	rhubarb
arbitrary	notorious	allure	miniature
summary	impervious	alliance	muscle

(3)

assistance	satchel	privilege	deceitfully
contrivance	separately	sergeant	defiantly
reluctance	successor	committee	effectively
remittance	mantelpiece	optician	possessively
reassurance	financial	guillotine	unbelievably

Dictation

To "lynch" and a "quisling" are also derivatives from personal names. The former comes from the notorious Judge Lynch who dispensed justice in the United States towards the end of the eighteenth century, and did so in such a summary and arbitrary manner that to be tried by him was virtually to be lynched. A quisling signifies someone who treacherously intrigues with a foreign power at the expense of his own country, and the word comes from Major Quisling, the renegade Norwegian officer who assisted the German Nazis in their invasion of Norway in 1940.

attendant	ancestor	realist	protestant
applicant	surveyor	egotist	attendance
assistant	professor	atheist	arrogance
immigrant	ambassador	scientist	accompanist
descendant	proprietor	humorist	ancestry

A. Fill each blank with the right noun from the box:

1. An — is a person who believes there is no God.
2. Anyone who faces the facts may be called a —.
3. An — is any of those from whom one is descended.
4. A person who applies for something is called an —.
5. — is a sign of too much pride.
6. The pianist who plays for a singer is called the —.
7. The — of a business is the person who owns it.
8. An — thinks and talks about himself too much.

B. Make more nouns ending in –or from these. Check your answers with the Little Dictionary.

1. execute
2. supervise
3. generate
4. profess
5. survey
6. conjure
7. compete
8. operate
9. elevate
10. war
11. impose
12. divide

C. Arrange each list in alphabetical order:

1. protestant, occupant, truant, tenant, merchant, migrant
2. typist, tourist, artist, atheist, mayor, motorist
3. amateur, ancestor, attendant, ambassador, assistance
4. combatant, consultant, claimant, contestant
5. industrialist, humorist, internationalist, inhabitant
6. conveyance, continuance, contrivance, countenance, compliance

A. Pronounce carefully the ou sound

1. as in rough, cuff (international phonetic symbol ʌ)
2. as in soup, moon (phonetic symbol u:)
3. as in journal, burn (phonetic symbol ə:)
4. as in ought, short (phonetic symbol ɔ:)
5. as in pout, now (phonetic symbol au)
6. as in soul, hold (phonetic symbol ou)

Each of the words below contains one of the above sounds. Arrange the words in six equal groups; number them 1–6, according to the sound they contain:

coupon	poultice	couple	boulder	naughty
lounge	foundry	coupé	bough	burly
tough	resource	scourge	nought	fussily
fought	courtesy	mourning	adjourn	booby
poultry	souvenir	county	coup	bowels
journey	courage	doughnut	country	wholly

B. Observe how the following words are translated into phonetic symbols:

cuff = kʌf caught = kɔ:t burn = bə:n round = raund
tough = tʌf rolled = rould room = ru:m shore = sɔ:

Now write the following in phonetic symbols:

1. taught 3. moon 5. found 7. core
2. fold 4. rough 6. turn 8. short

C. Give each numbered word its right antonym:

1. insert	rigid	7. summarize	mobile
2. interior	partly	8. static	obligatory
3. flexible	extract	9. connect	elaborate
4. colossal	expenditure	10. voluntary	frail
5. revenue	miniature	11. principal	subsidiary
6. wholly	exterior	12. burly	dissever

evade	intrude	erode	collide
evasion	intrusion	erosion	collision
dissuade	delude	corrode	deride
dissuasion	delusion	corrosion	derision
persuasion	seclusion	protrusion	incision

A. Notice that some verbs ending in –de change the d into s before adding –ion. Now make abstract nouns ending in –sion from these verbs:

1. collide
2. explode
3. include
4. delude
5. allude
6. dissuade
7. obtrude
8. corrode

B. Give the verbs from which these nouns come:

1. persuasion
2. collision
3. conclusion
4. division
5. exclusion
6. provision
7. derision
8. invasion

C. Use the right words from the box to complete these:

1. To remove the appendix the surgeon first makes an —.
2. Running water will — the surface of any earthen path.
3. He harboured a — as the result of being imposed upon.
4. The — of the iron bars by rust was aggravated by the damp.
5. His ideas were subjected to the — of mocking laughter.

D. Complete this table:

Verb	Noun	Adjective	Adverb
1. to elude	elusion	—	elusively
2. —	—	persuasive	persuasively
3. to deride	—	derisive	—
4. —	—	—	conclusively
5. —	—	provisional	provisionally

Study the meaning of the words in each group, and then use them to complete the sentences below :

disease, any particular form of illness
desist, to stop or leave off
decease, to die ; death

1. I must — from saying that the — of the boatswain was due to a — contracted as a result of the doctor's negligence, for it is by no means proved.

draft, to make a rough copy ; the rough copy itself
draught, a current of air
drought, a prolonged period with no rainfall

2. In the — of 1947, when no rain fell for thirty days, the old man decided to make a rough — of his will. But he sat in a — from the window and caught cold.

illusion, faulty perception that carries a wrong belief
elusion, the act of eluding or escaping
delusion, the fact of being imposed upon or deceived

3. As the result of an optical — a pool of water appeared in the desert. The traveller trudged on under the — that water was near. But, of course, it eluded him, and this — was tantalizing.

mechanic, skilled workman who makes or repairs machines
mechanical, to do with machines, working by machine [adj.]
mechanism, the structure of a machine

4. The works of a machine are called its —, and a — is needed to repair any — fault in it.

temperate, neither too hot nor too cold at any time
arid, dry and with very little vegetation
tropical, very hot and wet

5. He travelled through the vast — spaces of central Australia, to the — sugar belt along the coast of Southern Queensland, and then south to the — island of Tasmania.

canoeing	candour	incendiarism	convalescent
cantankerous	candidate	incandescent	convalescence
candelabra	candidature	crescent	adolescence
algebra	incense	adolescent	quiescence
orchestra	incendiary	reminiscent	effervescence

A. There are several dozen English words beginning with can–. This has no special significance, but facetiously we may call them " CAN " words. The CAN that puts himself forward for appointment, for example, is *candidate*. What are the following CANs ? Check your answers with the Little Dictionary.

    1. the CAN that is a large gun
    2. the CAN that is shrewd and worldly-wise
    3. the CAN that suggests sincerity
    4. the human CAN that eats human flesh
    5. the CAN that is a continuous bombardment
    6. the CAN that makes persons into saints
    7. the CAN that contains many candles
    8. the CAN that covers a throne or bed

B. More seriously, several of the CAN words derive from the Latin *candere* (to be shining white). Thus *candour* originally meant whiteness, since honesty and candour were thought of as being white and clean. A *candidate* was someone clothed in white, since candidates originally wore a white toga. To *incense* means to make white with rage. Now find four more derivatives from *candere* in the box, and try to explain how their meaning has evolved.

C. Make abstract nouns from these adjectives and define them :

1. candid   2. effervescent   3. quiescent   4. incandescent

expel	revert	comprehend	propulsion
expulsion	reversion	comprehensive	aversion
repulsion	conversion	reprehend	prehensile
compulsion	perversion	apprehensive	impregnable
compulsory	diversion	apprentice	impulsive

A. Complete these sentences with words from the box:

1. Monkeys have — tails.
2. There has to be a — of traffic when a road is impassable.
3. — people are apt to act suddenly without forethought.
4. They were safe within the castle as its walls were —.
5. I shall — Mr Blank, as our failure is due entirely to him.
6. The — person is fearful of what may happen.
7. It is a — to use your nose as a pincushion since that is not its proper use at all.
8. If you show an — from spelling, you literally are turning away from it in dislike.

B. To repel comes from the Latin prefix *re–* (back) and *pello* (I drive). It still has this meaning of to drive back. Now show the derivation and meaning of:

1. expel   2. dispel   3. propeller   4. repellent

C. All the words in the box are derived from the Latin verbs listed in the table below. Copy the table and insert all the words from the box.

1. *prehendo, prehensus* (seize) reprehension, apprehensive . . .
2. *verto, vertus* (turn) traverse, adversity, inversion . . .
3. *pello, pulsus* (drive) dispel, pulsation, propeller . . .

grotesque	indigent	diligence	emergency
grotesqueness	negligent	negligence	regency
picturesque	indulgent	divergence	pungency
statuesque	pungent	convergence	insurgency
burlesque	cogent	indigence	detergent

A. Make adjectives in –ent to correspond to these nouns :

1. intelligence   3. urgency   5. emergency   7. convergence
2. indigence   4. pungency   6. indulgence   8. regency

B. Use the right words from the box to complete these sentences :

1. She stood so still that she looked —.
2. Any cleansing agent may be called a —.
3. There is a — of our ways here, I going this way and you that.
4. An — takes place when the people rise in active revolt.
5. If anything is so comically distorted as to be ugly we call it —.

C. Notice how some adjectives ending in –ent change the t to ce when forming the corresponding noun. The noun often ends in –ence, though a few end in –ency. Now form the abstract nouns corresponding to these adjectives :

1. urgent   3. divergent   5. insurgent
2. negligent   4. convergent   6. pungent

D. Can you identify these GENTS ?

1. the convincing, forceful GENT
2. the GENT that is the opposite of divergent
3. the very needy GENT
4. the GENT that describes sharp, acrid, stinging smells
5. the GENT that rules

By far the greatest number of words that have enriched our vocabulary are Latin derivatives. Many of these have come directly from Latin books studied by scholars, especially during the Renaissance. Many also have come to us through French, since that language was largely derived from Latin and when the Norman Conquerors settled in England they brought with them many French terms that were readily absorbed by the native language. We have continued to borrow French and Latin words since those times. We have borrowed many words from Ancient Greek for our modern scientific terms too. Indeed, we have at intervals borrowed words from almost every other language in the world, particularly at those periods when we have been closely connected with a foreign language through trade, art or war. Thus when English nobles travelled to Italy during the Renaissance to learn music and painting, they brought back many Italian cultural words such as *contralto, piano, studio*; while contact with Dutch sailors and traders gave us *ballast, sloop, reef.* Here is a short list of words borrowed from other languages:

1. *Latin*: exit, pedestrian, terminus, contribution, apparatus
2. *Greek*: telephone, analysis, electricity, photograph
3. *Norman French*: leveret, venison, mutton, armour, judge, trespass
4. *Modern French*: etiquette, brochure, blonde, depot, précis
5. *Italian*: cartoon, intermezzo, opera, soprano, gondola
6. *Spanish*: alligator, cigar, El Dorado, flotilla, guerrilla
7. *Arabic*: alcohol, cipher, magazine, sherbet
8. *Dutch*: luff, boor, skipper, smack (boat), trigger

A. Copy out the list at the foot of the opposite page and then add to each line two words from the following italicized words. You will be able to guess most of them, but check all the derivations of the words by reference to an etymological dictionary.

specimen	*theatre*	*alphabet*	*junior*
brunette	*veal*	*brochure*	*verdict*
coffee	*yacht*	*smuggle*	*algebra*
serenade	*galleon*	*prima donna*	*mosquito*

B. Sometimes when a Norman French word was borrowed, the Old English word was not discarded. In this way we have synonyms like *purchase* (N.F.) and *buy* (O.E.). Pair each of the following Norman French words with its O.E. synonym:

N.F. 1. commence 2. testament 3. flower 4. desire 5. labour
O.E. bloom, work, begin, wish, will

C. Generally speaking, words that have been handed down from Old English are simpler and therefore better than those deriving from Latin or Greek. *Help* (O.E.) and *assistance* (L.) are synonymous. Yet when about to drown we do not shout, "assistance! assistance!" We shout "help! help!" The Old English word sounds more apt and expressive. Yet there might be a more formal occasion when the more pompous assistance would be preferable. We should therefore know both.

Give each numbered word on the left (L.) its synonym from the right (O.E.):

1. audacious	6. fraternity	end	wordiness
2. perspiration	7. terminate	spit	feelings
3. verbosity	8. onerous	bold	beseech
4. sentiments	9. expectorate	weighty	kind
5. benevolent	10. supplicate	sweat	brotherhood

When European explorers first visited the Canary Islands the most vivid memories they carried away were those of the wild dogs they had met there. Now, the Latin for a dog is *canis*, and consequently the islands were nicknamed the Canary Islands. Subsequently, the islands became famous not for dogs but for the yellow singing birds that were indigenous to them, coming from the Canaries. These birds became known as canaries. Thus we have the paradoxical fact of a small bird deriving its name from the Latin for a dog.

A. Consult a good dictionary to find the story behind:
1. daisy   2. sandwich   3. holiday   4. sun   5. volcano

B. As we saw on page 55, the simple Old English word is usually preferable; but there is sometimes a place for the longer word derived from Latin. Thus we might reasonably speak of a statesman being given a cordial reception at a formal banquet; but we should look very pompous and silly if we offered a close friend a cordial reception should he drop in for supper, when it would be more suitable to give him a warm welcome. Now find the Old English equivalent of each of these expressions deriving from Latin:

1. to commence operations	manly talk
2. virile conversation	a great fire
3. audacious belligerents	to speed the goods
4. a devoted consort	free wordiness
5. a conflagration	to begin work
6. gratuitous verbosity	to end right
7. to expedite the commodities	a loving wife
8. to terminate correctly	bold fighters

Unfortunately, English spelling is only partly phonetic. If it were wholly phonetic, each letter would represent one sound and one only, making the spelling of words extremely simple. In actual fact the one letter o, for example, may be used to represent at least seven distinct sounds, as you will observe from this list: oven, woman, women, tomb, colonel, police, comb. Consequently, the other way round, each sound may be represented by several different letters. Thus the single sound i as in *pit* may be spelt with twelve different letters or combination of letters:

1. i—grit, tribune	7. ia—carriage
2. a—village, furnace	8. ee—Greenwich
3. e—college, ages	9. ie—mischievous
4. u—busy, lettuce	10. y—rhythm, dynasty
5. ai—mountain, chaplain	11. ei—forfeit
6. ui—built, circuit	12. o—women

A. Copy the above list and add two more examples of each, except No. 12 for which there are no more.

B. In the same way, the sound of oo as in *boost* (phonetic symbol u:) may be spelt in nine different ways. There are two examples of each way in the list below. Sort them out and then make them into a table like the one above.

shrewd	brunette	roost	souvenir	canoe	jewellery
rumour	canoeist	ado	tomb	glue	aloof
cruise	eulogy	due	sleuth	coupon	bruise

C. Do the same with these, to show the five spellings of the sound of *a* as in *what* (phonetic symbol ɔ):

wattle	monarch	sausage	trough	cauliflower
cough	encore	yacht	rendezvous	competent

A. By looking up the meaning of the following words in the Little Dictionary, explain the force of each of the prefixes:

1. foreknowledge 3. subterranean 5. supersonic 7. prejudice
2. predetermine 4. extraordinary 6. contradict 8. emigrate

B. Write this list of italicized words and after each one write its synonym and antonym, to be chosen from those words following it:

1. *delete* : revise, pronounce, insert, erase, dilute
2. *adept* : skilled, adaptable, inexpert, adopted
3. *censure* : praise, centre, certify, scold, sense
4. *contemptuous* : contrary, disdainful, admiring, contemporary
5. *impartial* : prejudiced, imperial, impertinent, disinterested
6. *feasible* : contrivable, festive, fallible, impracticable
7. *flaunt* : float, flounder, display, foment, conceal
8. *ignoble* : ignorant, illustrious, disreputable, illuminated
9. *equanimity* : equality, composure, impatience, unanimity
10. *scepticism* : doubt, scaffolding, belief, scarcity, scenery
11. *fidelity* : treachery, fragility, fertility, loyalty
12. *inaugurate* : argue, incarcerate, terminate, initiate

C. We often use the names of creatures in expressions that have no literal connection with the creatures. Thus powder-monkeys were the boys who used to carry powder to the guns on board ship. Here are a dozen similar expressions. Complete them with the creatures' names.

1. a clothes —	frog		7. a round —	herring
2. the — share	bee		8. a — engine	bull
3. a — march	lion's		9. a — dozer	stag
4. a — jacket	crocodile		10. a — hole	robin
5. — tears	horse		11. a — party	pigeon
6. a — line	monkey		12. a red —	donkey

sagacity	elasticity	renounce	gauge
felicity	atrocity	relinquish	asphalt
simplicity	paucity	atrocious	picnicking
duplicity	domesticity	sagacious	carburettor
voracity	eccentricity	eccentric	pinnacle

A. Some eighty English words end in –city, and we may facetiously refer to them as CITIES. The CITY of quarrelsomeness will therefore be *pugnacity*. What are the following CITIES?

1. the CITY of happiness
2. the shrewd CITY
3. the CITY of home-life
4. the CITY of odd behaviour
5. the CITY of greediness
6. the simple CITY
7. the CITY of double-dealing
8. the CITY of small numbers and quantities

B. Very often words may be synonymous but have different uses. Thus hinder and obstruct are synonymous, but though we can obstruct a passage way, we cannot hinder it. Use the synonyms in brackets to complete the following:

1. The two boys — the cake into two and then —, one going to the cinema and the other to the swimming-pool. (separated, divided)
2. When he — his faith, he had to — his post in the church. (renounced, relinquish)
3. John — evil thoughts and looks an unpleasant character; but his brother — kind thoughts and looks a thoroughly likeable person. (harbours, cherishes)

C. Now write sentences to show the difference between:

1. abundance and exuberance
2. famous and notorious

The word *aster* comes ultimately from the Greek word meaning a star. The flower was so named because it looked like a star. An *asterisk* is a little star, and *astronomy* is the study of the stars. The Greek word is also concealed in *disaster*. This is made up of the noun *aster* and the prefix *dis–* meaning contrary to or against. Thus a disaster originally was something contrary to one's star, and this reminds us that in ancient times people believed that their destinies were controlled by the stars. We no longer subscribe to this superstition, but we nevertheless still talk about an ill-starred event.

Another superstition is embodied in *auspicious*, which comes from the Latin for a bird, *avis*, and from *spicere*, to look. The Romans believed that a soothsayer (*augur*) could foretell whether the future was bright by looking at the flight of birds. Hence an auspicious beginning is one that augurs well, since it begins under good auspices.

A. Try to find out what superstitious belief is embodied in the word *lunatic*.

B. Arrange the following words according to whether they derive from (1) *aster*, (2) *avis*, (3) *spicere*. Three of them may be placed in two lists each.

asterisk	auspicious	despicable	perspective
astrology	aviary	disastrous	spectacular
astronomical	aviator	frontispiece	speculate
auspices	conspicuous	inauspicious	star

channel	drivelling	leveller	evangelist
channelling	bevelled	cruellest	instrumentalist
tunnel	dishevelled	installation	immortalize
tunnelled	untravelled	chancellor	individualism
quarrelled	disembowelled	controllable	civilian

Note that the rule on page 18 needs qualification. When the suffix begins with a vowel, a final l preceded by a single vowel is usually doubled even when the accent does not fall on the last syllable. *E.g.* travel—traveller; panel—panelling. The main exceptions are parallel—paralleled and words taking the suffixes –ish –ism –ist –ize such as devilish, rationalism, vocalist, nationalize.

But remember that if the preceding vowel is a double one or the root word does not end in a single consonant, the l is not doubled. *E.g.* appeal—appealing; kneel—kneeler. A notable exception is wool—woollen.

A. Make words ending in –er, –ing and –ed from each of these:

1. quarrel   3. shovel   5. travel   7. signal
2. propel   4. retail   6. appeal   8. model

B. Five of the following words disobey the rule about doubling the final consonant as defined on page 18. Which are they and how do they disobey it?

1. submitting   3. marshalled   5. equalling   7. counsellor
2. referred   4. sniveller   6. rebellion   8. cancellation

C. Which of these are exceptions to the usual practice in doubling the final l? 1. coolest; 2. groveller; 3. metallic; 4. symbolic; 5. paralleled; 6. civilian; 7. blackmailer

flippant	substance	aridity	irresolute
diffuse	substantial	triviality	fluent
narrative	scrutiny	fertility	fluency
appearance	receptionist	solemnity	temporary
assault	conversationalist	cordiality	negligible

A. Give from the box the word meaning:

1. for the time being only
2. considerable in amount, or having real substance
3. so small that it can be neglected
4. smooth easy flow, especially in speech
5. spread out; not concentrated or to the point
6. close examination

B. Pair each noun phrase with its opposite on the right:

1. a trivial affair
2. a stubborn beast
3. a casual glance
4. an arid waste
5. a determined appearance
6. a concise narrative
7. a fluent talker
8. a substantial amount
9. a direct assault
10. a brisk promenade
11. a chilly reception
12. a temporary set-up
13. an impetuous remark
14. a spendthrift wife
15. a solemn observation

a fertile area
a diffuse story
a halting conversationalist
a serious matter
an oblique attack
a leisurely dawdle
a calculated comment
a prolonged scrutiny
a willing animal
a permanent arrangement
an irresolute air
a negligible quantity
a cordial welcome
a flippant remark
a thrifty spouse

depraved	precipitate	courtesy	disclosure
deprived	precocious	curtsy	erasure
scavenger	precarious	tacit	exposure
scapegoat	imminent	decrepit	censure
scaffold	eminent	decadent	enclosure

A. Choose the correct word from the brackets and write out each complete sentence:

1. The (scavenger, scapegoat, scaffold) bears the blame that should by rights be borne by others.

2. The refuse in the streets used to be cleared away by a (scapegoat, scaffold, scavenger).

3. The moral character of a (deprived, depraved, derived) person has become very bad.

4. I must return your bicycle because I do not wish you to be (depraved, derived, deprived) of its use.

5. A boy who is too knowing for his age is said to be (precocious, precipitate, precarious).

6. A (precarious, precipitate, precocious) action is one taken without enough forethought.

7. An (imminent, eminent) person stands out from the rest. An (imminent, eminent) event is one close at hand.

8. Your (curtness, curtsy, courtesy) in offering a seat to an elderly person will be much appreciated.

9. If a landlord allows his property to become (decrepit, tacit, courteous) he deserves the (disclosure, censure, erasure) of his tenants.

B. Now write sentences to bring out the use of:

1. disclosure   2. enclosure   3. tactful   4. tacit

The Latin for a body is *corpus* (*corporis*), and this word has a number of descendants in English. We see it in *corpse*, a dead body, and in a *corps*, a body of men in the army. Then a *corpulent* person is literally someone having a large body. To *incorporate* an idea in a composition, for example, means to bring it into the body of the composition. A *corporation*, on the other hand, is a group of people made legally into one body.

corps	capital	transmit	descend
corpse	decapitate	transmission	descent
corpulent	capitulate	missionary	descendant
incorporate	precipitate	missile	ascent
corporation	precipice	surmise	ascension

A. The words in the second list derive from *caput* (head); those in the third from *mittere, missus* (send); and those in the fourth from *scando, scansus* (climb). Copy the lists from the box and add to each list four words from the following:

condescend	corporate	captain	transcend
precipitous	scan	ascend	chapter
capitulation	corset	unremitting	commission
submissive	corporeal	corpuscle	committee

B. Explain the meaning of these words in such a way as to bring out the force of both the prefix and the Latin root:

1. transmit   2. descend   3. remission   4. committee

microbes	timpani	legacy	geology
leveret	pizzicato	executor	overture
selvedge	syllabus	acquittal	dyspepsia
pharmacy	insomnia	barrister	constellation
cuisine	diocese	intestate	psychology

Every sport, art, science, occupation has its own special vocabulary. We call such words *technical terms*. Sometimes there is another term used by the layman. Thus the biologist will talk about microbes, while you and I will call the same things germs. Microbe is a technical term. Timpani is a technical term of music, meaning what the layman usually calls kettledrums.

A. With the help of the Little Dictionary give the meaning of all the technical terms in the box. Arrange all twenty words in alphabetical order, and number them 1–20.

B. Now use the right words to complete these sentences:

1. Mr Brown received a — of £100 through the will of his employer.
2. — is the technical term for the style of cooking.
3. Mr Blank died — since he had made no will.
4. The study of the earth's crust is called —, and the study of the human mind is known as —.
5. Music is played — when the strings are plucked instead of a bow being used.
6. Stars forming an imaginary outline are known as a —.
7. One of the causes of — is —, making it wise to avoid eating rich food too soon before going to bed.

A. Here are lists for a spelling-bee:

Place Adjectives	Literary	Teasers	French
Portuguese	abbreviation	siege	amateur
Norwegian	paraphrase	almanac	etiquette
Bohemian	alphabetical	rhythm	nonchalance
Venetian	monologue	wholly	reservoir
Genoese	colloquial	ukulele	souvenir
Neapolitan	asterisk	schedule	rendezvous
Sicilian	anthology	plebiscite	bureau
Maltese	vernacular	eczema	naive
Afghan	parenthesis	jodhpurs	liqueur
Egyptian	memoir	anniversary	connoisseur

B. How much of each of these series can you complete?

1. abbreviation, botheration, celebration, determination . . .
2. alphabetical, botanical, cordial, decimal, educational . . .
3. angular, beggar, circular, dissimilar . . .
4. Alsatian, barbarian, civilian, Devonian, Etonian . . .

C. Group these words in five equal classes of:

1. *Virtues* 2. *Smells* 3. *Travellers* 4. *Vehicles* 5. *Light*

fragrance	discretion	integrity	co-operativeness
voyagers	conveyance	aroma	excursionists
ambulance	tourists	shimmer	perfume
incandescence	illumination	omnibus	luminosity
veracity	odour	passengers	limousine

D. Find five words to place in each of the following classes. You may only use words listed in the Little Dictionary.

1. *vices*　　　2. *receptacles*　　　3. *occupations*　　　4. *instruments*

paragraph	gramophone	telescope	speedometer
telegraph	saxophone	microscope	barometer
autograph	homophone	periscope	thermometer
photograph	microphone	stethoscope	cyclometer
seismograph	xylophone	stereoscope	micrometer

A. With the help of the Little Dictionary, write definitions of all the words in the box, arranging them alphabetically and numbering them 1–20.

B. Now choose from the following definitions the meaning of each of these Greek endings: 1. –graph; 2. –phone; 3. –scope; 4. –meter:

instrument for observation   sound or voice
measuring instrument   something written

C. On the right are the instruments, and on the left are the people who use them. Write a sentence linking the two. Begin like this: 1. The policeman uses a truncheon.

1. policeman	5. whaler	forceps	microscope
2. conductor	6. biologist	telescope	truncheon
3. surgeon	7. mechanic	harpoon	stethoscope
4. astronomer	8. doctor	baton	spanner

D. With the help of the Little Dictionary distinguish between the following homophones, beginning like this: 1. Any corn is a cereal, but a serial is a story given in instalments.

| 1. serial | 2. sealing | 3. horde | 4. stationery |
| cereal | ceiling | hoard | stationary |

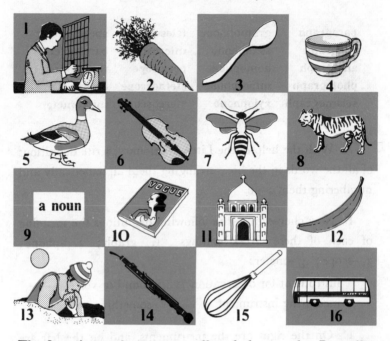

The first picture shows a post-office clerk at work. Post-office clerks belong to that class of people called white-collar workers. His label would therefore be " a white-collar worker ". Now write out the following labels in the same order as the pictures they go with. If in difficulty, consult any good dictionary.

a piece of cutlery   a root vegetable

a piece of crockery   a stinging insect

a petrol-driven vehicle   a web-footed bird

a place of worship   a kitchen utensil

a string instrument   a monthly periodical

a wood-wind instrument   a white-collar worker

a manual worker   a quadruped

a tropical fruit   a part of speech

bonus, payment made in addition to what is due
bribe, money offered to get something done, often unlawful
fine, sum of money paid as a punishment
gratuity, small present of money for good service ; a tip
increment, amount by which a payment increases
pension, payment received after retiring from work
ransom, price demanded before a captive is set free
rates, tax levied on property by local council
salary, fixed pay for regular work when paid by the year
surtax, tax in addition to income tax levied on incomes above
  a certain amount
wage, amount paid weekly for work done

The nouns defined above all name payments of money, and **yet each** payment is quite different. Study the differences, and **then use** each noun to complete one of the following sentences.

1. As well as paying income tax, Mr Prosper paid — on all that he earned above £2,500 a year.
2. Mr Jones has retired from work on a — of £7 a week.
3. The manager was paid a — of £2,000 a year.
4. The cyclist was ordered to pay a — of £5 for riding without a rear light.
5. We pay £60 a year to the Council as — on our house.
6. The French knight held Sir Aubrey prisoner for a — of £800.
7. The gardener was paid a — of £10 a week.
8. The cheat offered the umpire a — of £10 to declare him the winner.
9. At Christmas the staff received a — of an extra week's wages.
10. She left a — of 50p for the hotel porter to show that she was pleased with the way in which he had helped her.
11. His salary went up by an — of £50 each year.

A. Add –ence or –ance to make a word of each of the following. Check carefully with the Little Dictionary.

1. disobedi–   3. annoy–   5. resili–   7. conveni–   9. compli–
2. acquaint–   4. arrog–   6. occurr–   8. admitt–   10. leni–

B. In the same way add –or or –er to each of these :

1. incubat–   3. ancest–   5. accelerat–   7. carri–   9. propriet–
2. loiter–   4. debt–   6. baromet–   8. default–   10. success–

C. Give each of these its synonym from the list in italics :

1. solitary   4. tranquillize   7. dissolve   10. anonymous
2. illegible   5. invariable   8. retort   11. conversation
3. feign   6. parenthesis   9. succumb   12. peculiarities

calm	*nameless*	*dialogue*	*rejoinder*
melt	*lonely*	*pretend*	*unreadable*
brackets	*oddities*	*constant*	*submit*

D. In the same way give each of these its antonym :

1. ancestor   4. candour   7. pessimist   10. substantial
2. attendance   5. subtract   8. credible   11. diffuse
3. theoretical   6. gradual   9. persuade   12. arid

secretiveness	*absence*	*add*	*dissuade*
unbelievable	*sudden*	*practical*	*concentrated*
descendant	*luxuriant*	*optimist*	*negligible*

E. Explain the meaning of each of these words in such a way as to bring out the contribution made by the prefix:

1. expulsion   2. transport   3. postscript   4. superfluous

F. What changes have taken place in the root words from which these come ?

1. measurable   3. daisies   5. monstrous   7. reparable
2. preferring   4. vicious   6. identified   8. stability

1. the owner of a business   (page 47)
2. a turning away in dislike   (52)
3. the tidal mouths of great rivers   (9)
4. to impose upon or deceive   (49)
5. the science of directing great military operations   (25)
6. one who has come into a country to live   (47)
7. smooth easy flow, especially in speech   (62)
8. warm and friendly because coming from the heart   (7)

9. inclined to neglect one's duty   (53)
10. to say or do something without preparation   (30)
11. to laugh to scorn   (49)
12. without having made a will   (65)
13. difficult or impossible in practice   (15)
14. to break off in order to start again later   (48)
15. an elected representative sent to a conference   (33)
16. fine and delicate and therefore difficult to appreciate   (11)

17. neither too hot nor too cold at any time   (50)
18. instrument for observing sounds in the chest   (67)
19. to rebuke or find fault with   (52)
20. not fit to be chosen   (37)
21. comically distorted   (53)
22. one fond of conversation   (62)
23. a group of stars forming an imaginary outline   (65)
24. the fact of being deceived or imposed upon   (50)

25. to take the place of   (38)
26. the giving off of bubbles of gas   (51)
27. to decide beforehand   (58)
28. to surrender on terms (i.e. under headings)   (64)
29. just about to happen   (63)
30. a pamphlet or a few leaves stitched together   (54)
31. recalling past things   (51)
32. the fact of tending to meet in a point   (53)

Third Spelling Test

(1)

nuisance	recital	conversion	chorus
anxious	observant	reversion	character
yacht	advisable	perversion	chronic
woollen	fascinating	dimension	aching
patience	subtly	convulsion	chaotic

(2)

ennoble	deficient	eventually	immerse
errand	deficiency	possessively	immigrant
effectively	efficiency	temporarily	innocent
essential	emergency	contemptibly	irritate
erroneous	currency	apparently	irresistible

(3)

participate	benefited	librarian	accompanied
participation	mis-spelling	guardian	appalling
anticipation	controlling	pedestrian	worshipper
exhilaration	regrettable	electrician	miscellaneous
immigration	paralleled	physician	embarrassment

Dictation

The accepted meanings of English words are chronically disinclined to remain static, and in the course of time may be fundamentally altered. Thus, to explode originally meant to drive away by clapping and was the opposite of to applaud. Similarly, an idiot was merely a man who did not take part in public life. Gradually, however, it came to signify someone incapable of participating in it, and so eventually someone mentally deficient. This tendency towards change may appear regrettable, but it is in the nature of language, and therefore irresistible.

THE LITTLE DICTIONARY

abbreviate, to shorten when referring to words

abstract, considered apart from any application to a particular object; not concrete

abundance, (from the Latin *abundare,* to overflow), great quantity; plenty; more than enough

academic, scholarly

accede, to enter upon an office or dignity

accelerator, thing that causes an increase in speed

accidental, the opposite of deliberate; done by accident

accompanist, the pianist who plays for a singer

accompany, to play for a singer; to go along with

accomplice, person who aids another in crime

accountant, person who inspects accounts professionally

accumulate, to gather; to collect

accurate, exact; precise; correct

acquaintance, knowledge of person or thing

acquiesce, to accept conclusions, arrangements, etc.

acquit, to declare not guilty. So **acquittal,** a setting free by declaring not guilty

addicted, strongly inclined

adjacent, near; adjoining

adjourn, to break off in order to start again later

adjutant, the officer who assists a commanding officer

admittance, right of entering

advent, coming; arrival

affection, a feeling towards one you love

affix, to fix or fasten to or on

afflicted, troubled; distressed

aggravate, to make worse or more severe

alms, money or gifts to help the poor

amateur, person who does something for pleasure; the opposite of a professional

ambulance, vehicle for conveying wounded or injured persons

ammunition, bullets, shells, powder for weapons

ampersand, the sign (&) that means *and*

amplify, to make fuller; to give in more detail

ancestor, person from whom one is descended

annoyance, vexation

annuity, sum of money paid every year

anoint, to put oil on

anonymous, of unknown name

antiquity, oldness; times long past

antonym, word of opposite meaning

anxiety, uneasiness; fear of what may happen

apathetic, indifferent; showing no enthusiasm

applause, approval loudly expressed

applicant, person who applies for something

apprehensive, anxious; worried; afraid

aquiline, of or like an eagle; hooked like an eagle's beak

aria, melody for a single voice, especially in opera

arid, dry and with very little vegetation

armistice, temporary stop in fighting, by agreement

armour, protective covering

aroma, fragrance ; sweet smell

arrogance, too much pride ; haughtiness

ascetic, refraining from pleasures and comforts

assailant, attacker

assiduous, attentive ; careful ; diligent

assign, to make over ; to give as a share

astronomer, expert in astronomy, the science of the heavenly bodies

athiest, person who believes there is no God

attract, to draw to oneself

audience, assembly of listeners ; persons within hearing

authorize, to give right or power to do something

autograph, (from the Greek *autos,* self, and *graphein,* to write), person's handwriting or signature

avenue, way of approach ; wide street ; roadway bordered by trees

aversion, strong dislike

baptism, a dipping into or sprinkling with water as a Christian sign. So to **baptize**

barometer, (from the Greek *baros,* weight), instrument for measuring atmospheric pressure (weight of the air) and used for forecasting the weather

barrel, wooden container with round flat ends and curved sides hooped with metal ; tube of a gun

barrister, member of the legal profession who has been admitted to the bar and can plead in any court

bassoon, wooden double-reed instrument used as bass to the oboe

baton, stick used by conductor of orchestra etc., for beating time

becalm, tó prevent from moving by lack of wind

benefactor, person who does a good deed

beneficial, producing good ; helpful

benevolent, desirous of doing good ; well-wishing

benumb, to cause to lose the power of feeling

bereavement, loss of someone dear to you

biceps, (two-headed, from the Latin), front muscle with double head between shoulder and elbow

biennial, lasting two years

bier, movable stand on which coffin is taken to grave

biologist, expert in biology, the science of life or living things

biped, animal with two feet, as man and birds

biscuit, (twice cooked, from the Latin), thin flour-cake baked until very dry and crisp

bisect, to divide into two parts

bombardier, artillery non-commissioned officer below sergeant

brochure, (from the French *brocher,* to stitch), printed and stitched book containing only a few leaves ; pamphlet

brook, small stream

bursar, treasurer of a college

calibre, inside diameter of a gun barrel

camouflage, disguise of objects to deceive the enemy

Canada, British Dominion near U.S.A.

Canberra, capital of Australia

candelabra, large ornamental candlestick having several branches

candid, sincere; frank

candidate, person who puts himself forward for appointment. Hence **candidature,** being a candidate; standing for election

candour, sincerity; frankness

cannibal, eater of human flesh

cannon, large gun

cannonade, continuous firing of cannons; bombardment

canny, shrewd; worldly-wise

canonization, the act of canonizing, adding a dead person's name to the list of saints, known as the canon

canopy, covering fixed over throne, bed, etc.

capitulate, to surrender on certain terms or conditions, usually drawn up under several heads

carrier, person or thing that carries something

cascade, small waterfall

casualties, persons killed or injured in accidents or war

cataract, large, steep waterfall

cavalier, horseman; mounted soldier

ceiling, inside top covering of a room

censure, unfavourable opinion; expression of disapproval

cereal, corn or grain used as food

ceremonial, formal; having to do with ceremony

chaperon, married or elderly woman in charge of girl on social occasion

chastise, to beat; to punish

circuitous, roundabout; not direct

circular, shaped like a circle

cleavage, split; division; way in which a thing tends to be split

cogent, (of argument etc.), forceful; convincing

collapsible, able to be collapsed

collier, coal-miner; ship carrying coal

colonel, officer commanding a regiment

combustible, capable of burning

committee, group of persons appointed or elected to do certain things committed to them, i.e. delivered into their charge

commodities, articles of trade

communist, person who supports a system of public ownership

comparable, able to be compared; similar

comparative, the second degree of comparison (positive, comparative, superlative)

competitor, person who competes; rival

compliance, act of complying; act of yielding to another's wishes

compliment, pleasing word or act; expression of regard

compromise, to settle a dispute by each side giving up part of demands

conceited, having too high an opinion of oneself

concession, act of admitting or granting

concord, agreement; harmony

confluent, flowing together; uniting (of rivers etc.)

conjecture, to form an opinion without sufficient proof

conjunction, act of joining together

conjuror, person who performs conjuring tricks by clever movements of his hands

consciousness, quality of being aware or of knowing

conspiracy, act of conspiring; agreement to do wrong; plot

constellation, group of stars forming an imaginary outline

contagion, spread of disease by contact. So **contagious**

contemplative, given to looking at or thinking about things for a long time

contemporary, belonging to the same time

contradict, to speak against; to say the opposite of

contravene, to go against; to infringe; to violate

controversy, (turning against), argument on subject about which different opinions exist

convene, to gather together; to assemble (of persons)

convenience, (coming together), quality of being **convenient**, i.e. suitable, handy, well arranged, easy to use

convention, gathering; assembly (of persons)

convergence, (turning towards), tendency to meet in a point. So **convergent**, as of two lines meeting in a point

conversationalist, person fond of or good at conversation

conveyance, act of carrying; thing or vehicle that carries persons or goods

co-operate, to work together. So **co-operative** and **co-operativeness**, willingness to work with others

cordial, of the heart; warm and friendly

corporal, belonging to the body

correspond, to fit; to suit; to be similar *to*; to exchange letters *with*

corrode, to eat away gradually. So **corrosion**

corrugate, to contract into ridges, wrinkles or folds

courageous, brave

courtesy, polite behaviour

covetous, eager to obtain and be possessed of

creditable, bringing credit, honour or praise

crevasse, deep split in the ice of a glacier

crucial, very important

cuisine, style of cooking

cyclometer, (from the Greek *kuklos*, circle), instrument recording revolutions of a wheel

dais, raised platform, especially for seat like a throne

debar, to bar or shut out; to prevent

debtor, person who owes something to another

decease, to die; death

decrepit, broken down with age

default, to fail in duty. So **defaulter**

defer (carry apart), to delay; to put off

defer (bring down), to give way to the wishes or opinions of another. So **deference**, compliance; courteous submission

delegate, elected representative sent to a conference

deliberation, slowness and care in doing or thinking

delinquent, offending; guilty of a fault

delude, to impose upon or deceive. So **delusion**, the fact of being deluded

deprave, to make bad or worse; to debase

deprive, to take away from

deride, to laugh to scorn; to make fun of. So **derision**

derrick, contrivance for hoisting heavy weights

descend, to climb down; to go or come down. So **descent**

desist, to stop; to leave off

detergent, cleansing (agent)

detract (draw from), to take away from; reduce the credit due to

diffuse, spread out; not concentrated or to the point

diocese, district over which a bishop has jurisdiction

directory, book of names and addresses

disarmament, reduction of military force

disarray, to throw into disorder or confusion

disclosure, thing disclosed, uncovered, revealed or made known

discord, want of concord or agreement

discretion, good judgment; care in speech or action

discriminate, to see or make a difference between

disease, any particular form of illness

disgruntled, discontented; in a bad humour

disintegrate, to break up; to separate into small pieces

dismember, to separate the members or limbs from each other; to pull to pieces

disobedience, refusal to obey; disregard of orders

dispassionate, free from emotion or prejudice

dispel (drive from), to drive in different directions; to disperse (fears etc.)

disperse, to scatter; to go or send into different parts

disreputable not respectable in character or appearance

dissent, disagreement in opinion

dissident, disagreeing; at variance

dissolution, disintegration; act of dissolving or breaking up

dissuade, to advise against; to persuade not to do

distract (draw away), to pull in different directions; to divert (attention, the mind, etc.)

divergence, act of going in different directions; opposite of convergence

diversion, turning aside; diverting

divisor, number by which another is divided

domesticity, home life

dormitory, sleeping-room containing a number of beds

draft, to make a rough copy; the rough copy itself

draught, a current of air

draughts, game played on a chess-board

drought, prolonged period with no rainfall

duplicator, machine for making exact copies of anything written or typed

duplicity, deceitfulness; double-dealing

Dutch, of or having to do with Holland (the Netherlands)

dyspepsia, indigestion

eccentricity, odd behaviour

effervescence, the commotion of a liquid produced by the escape of gas. So **effervescent**

effluent, flowing out or forth, as of a stream from another

egotist, person who thinks and talks about himself too much

eject, to throw out; to drive away

elevator, machine for raising to a higher floor; a lift

elusion, act of escaping adroitly from blow, grasp, danger, etc.

embezzlement, theft of money entrusted to one's care

emigrate, to go to another country and settle down there

eminent, exalted; distinguished; standing out from the rest

emotions, strong feelings of love, joy, etc.

enclosure, space or ground enclosed or fenced in; anything enclosed with a letter in an envelope

endorse, (from the Latin *dorsum*, the back), to confirm a document by signing on the back of it. So **endorsement**

entity, thing's existence as opposed to its qualities; thing that has real existence

envelop, to wrap up or surround

epilogue, (from the Greek meaning "to say in addition"), conclusion of a literary work; speech or short poem addressed by actor to audience at end of play

erode, to eat away

estuary, mouth of river up which the tide runs

event (that which comes out), happening. So **eventual,** coming as a consequence, and **eventually**

excavate, to dig out, leaving a hole

exclusion, shutting out

excursion, pleasure trip by a number of persons. So **excursionists**

executor, person appointed by testator to execute his will

exempt (take out), to free from. So **exempt** (adj.), freed from; not liable to. So **exemption,** freedom from an obligation

expectancy, state of looking forward to

expel, to drive out of or from; to force to leave (school etc.)

experience, knowledge or skill gained by practice

expulsion, state of being expelled

extract, to draw out. So **extracting**

extraordinary, out of the ordinary; not in the usual course

exuberant, (from the Latin *ex*, out, and *uberare*, to be fruitful), abounding; overflowing with health, spirit, good nature, etc. So **exuberance**

facilitate, to make easy

faint, to lose consciousness; to swoon

famous, celebrated; well known

farcical, appropriate to farce; ludicrous

fatality, death by accident or war

feat, noteworthy act of valour

feelings, sympathies; emotions; state of mind

feign, to pretend; to put on false appearance of

felicity, happiness

feline, of or belonging to the cat family; catlike

feminine, marking the gender of the female sex

feudalism, custom in the Middle Ages of giving military and other services in exchange for use of land

fibre, substance composed of thread-like tissue—wool, flax, etc.

Finnish, of or having to do with Finland

florist, person who sells or cultivates flowers

fluent, flowing smoothly and easily, especially in speech

forceps, surgical pincers

foreknowledge, knowledge of something before it happens

fragrance, sweet smell

fraternize, to make friends with

fresh, new; additional; not stale

fruiterer, person who sells fruit

garrison, soldiers stationed in a town to defend it

gasometer, container for holding and measuring gas; gasholder

gauntlet, stout glove with long wrist

generator, apparatus for producing electricity etc.

genial, cheerful; friendly

geology, study of the earth's crust

gesticulate, to make gestures

Ghanaian, of or having to do with Ghana (capital Accra)

gramophone, instrument for recording and reproducing sounds

-graph, suffix from the Greek *graphein,* to write

grazier, person who fattens cattle for market

grotesque, so comically distorted as to be ugly

guerrilla (or **guerilla,** from the Spanish meaning " little warfare "), irregular war waged by small bodies acting independently

guiltless, not guilty; innocent

harass, to vex or worry by repeated attacks

harpoon, spear with rope attached used for catching whales

hoard, stock laid up; hidden supply

homophone, (from the Greek *homos,* same), word sounding like another but with different spelling and meaning

honesty, uprightness; truthfulness

horde, troop of nomads; crowd; swarm

humorous, the opposite of serious

hurriedly, in a hurried or hasty fashion

hypnotize, to put into a state resembling deep sleep

ignore, to take no notice of

illegal, not allowed by law

illegible, not legible ; not able to be read

illiterate, (from the Latin *in,* not, and *literatus,* learned, from *litera,* a letter), unable to read

illumination, that which gives light

illusion, faulty perception that carries a wrong belief

illustrate (throw light on), to make clear by pictures or examples

immigrant, person who has come into a country to live

imminent, just about to happen

immobile, not able to move

immortalize, to make undying ; to confer undying fame upon

immunity, freedom from punishment, disease, etc.

imperceptible, so small as not to be perceived ; very slight or gradual

imperturbable, able to keep calm under great excitement

impostor, deceiver ; person who imposes upon by professing to be what he is not

impracticable, difficult or impossible in practice

impregnable, not to be taken by assault ; unconquerable

improvise, to compose, speak or entertain without preparation

impulsive, apt to act suddenly without forethought

impunity, exemption from punishment

incandescent, glowing with heat ; shining brightly. So **incandescence**

incendiary, (from the Latin *incendiarius,* that causes fire), pertaining to the malicious burning of property ; person guilty of this. So **incendiarism,** arson

incense, (from the Latin *incendere,* to set on fire or inflame), to enrage, to make angry

incision, cut made by a sharp instrument

incomprehensible, not able to be understood

incubator, apparatus for hatching chicks

indebted, owing money or gratitude

indestructible, not able to be destroyed

indigent, poor ; needy. So **indigence**

ineligible, not eligible ; not fit to be chosen

infantry, foot soldiers

iniquity, wickedness ; gross injustice

initial, coming first

insanitary, (from the Latin *sanitas,* health), not sanitary ; unhealthy

inscription, words written on monument, coin, etc.

insidious, treacherous ; crafty ; working secretly

insignia, distinguishing signs (emblems, badges, etc.) of high position

insomnia, sleeplessness

insurgent, rising in active revolt. So **insurgency**

integrity, honesty ; uprightness

interior, inside ; inner part

intervene, to come between so as to influence the result. So **intervention**

intestate, without having made a will. So **to die intestate**

invalid, person who is ill

invalid, not valid; having no legal force

invent, (from the Latin *invenire*, to come upon), to find or find out; to discover. So **inventor,** person who invents

involuntary, not voluntary; not done of one's own free will. So **involuntarily**

irresistible, not able to be resisted; carrying all before it

irrigation, act of supplying land with water (from " to irrigate ")

itinerary, (from the Latin *itinerarius*, belonging to or concerning a journey), route taken on a journey; record of travel; guide-book

jet, (from the Latin *jactere*, to throw), a spout of water

jocular, given to joking

journalism, business of managing, editing or writing for journals or newspapers

knave, rascal; lowest court card in each suit, often called **jack**

laboratory, place in which scientific and experimental work is done

lagoon, stretch of salt water separated from sea by sandbanks or coral reef

lake, large expanse of water surrounded by land

larceny, theft

latterly, in late or recent times

legacy, sum of money or article given by will

lenience, quality of being gentle and indisposed to severity

leveret, young hare

lieutenant, officer next below captain

limousine, old-fashioned type of motor-car

loiter, to linger on the way. So **loiterer**

luminosity, the quality of being luminous, emitting or full of light

lunar, of the moon; resembling the moon

lunatic, (from the Latin *luna*, the moon), insane person, once supposed to be influenced by the moon

luscious, richly sweet in taste or smell; very delicious

macaroni, long tubes of wheaten paste used as food

magistrate, civil officer with power to apply the law; justice of the peace

malice, active ill-will. So **malicious,** bearing malice; having vindictive feelings

Maltese, of or having to do with Malta

manacle, handcuff; fetter for the hands

mannequin, woman who earns a living by wearing and showing off clothes

manœuvre, planned movement of troops or ships of war

manuscript, book or document written by hand

martial, to do with war

masculine, marking the gender of the male sex

mechanic, skilled workman who makes or repairs machines. So **mechanical,** of machines; **mechanism,** structure of machine

menial, appropriate to a servant

-meter, suffix from the Greek *metron,* a measure

metric, according to the decimal system of weights and measures

microbe, (from the Greek for for " small life "), minute living organism causing disease etc.; germ

micrometer, instrument for measuring very small distances etc.

microphone, instrument for intensifying small sounds

microscope, instrument for viewing very small objects

milliner, person who makes or sells women's hats

miraculous, like a miracle; contrary to the laws of nature

mischievous, naughty

mis-shapen, badly shaped; deformed

modest, without too high an opinion of oneself. So **modesty**

modify, to make partial changes in

monologue, (from the Greek meaning " speaking alone "), a dramatic composition for a single performer

mutual, given and received to a like extent, e.g. mutual dislike, mutual affection

negligent, inclined to neglect one's duty

negligible, so small that it can be neglected

new, not existing before; fresh

notorious, well known in a bad sense, e.g. a notorious pirate

now, at this moment

obedience, willingness to do as one is told

oboe, wooden double-reed instrument used as treble to the bassoon

occurrence, happening; event

odour, smell, either pleasant or unpleasant

omnibus, public vehicle for conveying passengers

operator, person who operates machine etc.

optician, maker or seller of optical instruments

optimist, person who looks on the bright side of things

orchid, beautiful flower

overture, musical piece played as introduction to an opera

pacifism, opposition to war

paragraph, (from the Greek *para,* at the side, and *graphein,* to write), originally the symbol ¶ to call attention to new section; now distinct part of chapter etc., indicated by indentation of first line

passenger, traveller in public conveyance

patriotism, love of one's country and devotion to its welfare

paucity, smallness of number or quantity

penitence, state of being sorry or repentant

perfume, sweet smell

periscope, (from the Greek *peri,* around, and *skopein,* to see), apparatus enabling person in submarine to obtain view above surface of water

THE LITTLE DICTIONARY (85)

perpendicular, at right angles to plane of horizon

persevere, to persist; to continue steadily at difficult task

perversion, turning to wrong end; putting to wrong use

pessimist, person who looks on the gloomy side of things

pharmacy, preparation and dispensing of drugs; chemist's shop

-phone, suffix from the Greek *phone*, sound

photograph, (from the Greek *phos photos*, light, and *graphein*, to write), picture taken with a camera

piety, quality of being devout or religious

piper, person who plays a pipe

pizzicato, (Italian for " pinched "), effect produced by plucking string of violin etc. instead of using bow

polar, to do with North and South Poles

polygamy, practice of having more than one wife at a time

pond, body of still water not so large as lake and usually artificially formed

pool, small body of still water, usually of natural formation

populous, thickly populated; having many inhabitants

Portuguese, of or having to do with Portugal

postscript, (from the Latin *postscriptum*, written after), addition to a letter after it has been written and signed

potential, capable of coming into being or action

precede, to go before in time, rank, importance, etc.

precipitate, headlong; hasty; done without thought

precocious, ripe before the usual time; developing prematurely

predetermine, to decide beforehand

prehensile, (from the Latin *prehendere*, to lay hold of, seize), capable of grasping or wrapping around, as is a monkey's tail

prejudice (judgment before), opinion formed without full knowledge; preconceived opinion; bias

premier, chief; first; prime minister

preside (sit before), to sit in a place of power or authority; to have charge of a meeting

pretentious, full of pretence; arrogant; doing things for show

prevent (come before), to hinder; to keep from doing

previous, (from the Latin *prae*, before, and *via*, a way), going before in time; prior

principal, first in rank or importance

prodigal, spending extravagantly; squandering

prodigy, marvellous thing, especially one out of the course of nature. So **prodigious**

professor, head teacher in college or university

propeller (driver forward), screw of steamship

proprietor, owner of a business

protracted (drawn forth), drawn out; prolonged

psychology, science of the human mind or soul

puddle, small pool of dirty water

pungent, (from the Latin *pungere*, to prick), sharply affecting organs of smell and taste. So **pungency**

qualm, sudden disturbing feeling in the mind

quiescent, quiet; motionless; inert. So **quiescence**

rationally, in a reasoned way

realist, person who faces the facts

rebut, to force back; to disprove a statement, charge, etc.

recant, (from the Latin *recantare*, to sing again), to take back a statement or opinion; to retract

reconcilable, able to be reconciled; able to be settled or agreed

reconnaissance, examination of a tract of country

reconnoitre, to make a survey of enemy's position and strength

recruit, newly enlisted soldier

refrigerator, place for keeping food cool

refugee, person who flees for safety

refute, to disprove and overthrow by argument, evidence or proof

regent, person who rules in place of absent or unfit monarch. So **regency**

rejoinder, what is said in reply

relegate, to send down or away; to consign to an inferior position

relinquish, to give up; to abandon

reminiscent, recalling past things

remission, (from the Latin *remittere*, to send back, relax), forgiveness of sin etc.; pardon; diminution or lessening

reparable, able to be repaired or made good

repel, to drive back; to be repulsive or distasteful to. So **repellent**

reprehend, (from the Latin *reprehendere*, to hold back, seize, check), to blame; to rebuke; to find fault with. So **reprehension**

reservoir, place where water is stored for use

residue, that which remains after part is taken away

resilience, elasticity; power to resume original shape after stretching or compression

retailer, person who buys from the wholesaler and resells to the customer

retort, sharp reply

retract, to draw back; to withdraw what has been said

revenue, that which comes back as income or profit

rivulet, small stream

sagacity, quickness of understanding; soundness of judgment

salvage, payment made for saving ship or cargo from loss; rescue of property from fire etc. So **to salvage**

satchel, small bag for carrying books etc.

saxophone, brass wind instrument with finger keys, named after its inventor, Adolphe Sax

scabbard, sheath of sword etc.

scapegoat, person bearing blame due to others

scavenger, person employed to clean streets by collecting and carrying away refuse

-scope, suffix from the Greek *skopein*, to see

science, system of facts and principles concerning any subject

score, the number twenty

scrutiny, close examination

sealing, act of stamping with a seal

sedentary, involving much sitting

sedition, agitation directed against authority of the state

selvedge, edge of cloth woven so that it cannot unravel

seismograph, instrument for recording tremors caused by earthquakes

sergeant, non-commissioned officer ranking above corporal

serial, story published in instalments

shimmer, faint gleam or shine

simplicity, the quality of being simple

smack, sloop for fishing

solar, to do with the sun

spanner, instrument for turning nut on screw

spectacular, making a great display

spectator, person who looks on

speedometer, instrument indicating speed of motor vehicle

stationary, not moving; remaining in one place

stationery, writing paper, envelopes, etc.

statuesque, resembling a statue in dignity or beauty

stellar, concerning the stars

stereoscope, (from the Greek *stereos*, solid, and *skopein*, to see), optical instrument giving the effect of three dimensions to a flat image

stethoscope, (from the Greek *stethos*, breast, and *skopein*, to see), instrument for observing sounds in the chest

strategy, science of directing great military operations

subaltern, any commissioned officer below the rank of captain

subside, to settle down or sink in level. So **subsidence**

substantial, having substance; real; considerable in amount

subterranean, below the surface of the earth; underground

subtle, fine; delicate; difficult to appreciate

subtraction (drawing back), act of taking away one number from another

succumb, to be overcome; to give way; to yield

superannuate, (from the Latin *super*, over, above, and *annus*, a year), to send person into retirement with a pension

superflous (flowing over), more than enough; not needed

superlative, the third degree of comparison (positive, comparative, superlative)

supersede (sit above), to take the place of

supersonic (beyond sound), travelling faster than sound

superstructure, that part of a building above the foundations

supervisor, person who supervises; overseer

supine, lying face upward; indolent; listless

surveyor, person who surveys land etc.

swoon, to faint

syllabus, complete set of courses for study

sympathize, to feel or express sympathy

synonym, word having same meaning as another. So **synonymous,** having same meaning

tacit, (from the Latin *tacitus,* silent), implied but not expressed in words, as tacit consent or agreement

tactful, having tact; able to say or do the right thing

tan, brown colour of person's skin through exposure to sun

tear, drop of salty liquid from the eye

tele-, Greek prefix meaning " afar off "

telegraph (*graphein,* to write), apparatus for sending signals or messages to a distance

telescope (*skopein,* to see), instrument for making distant objects appear nearer or larger

television, transmission of visual images by radio

temperate, neither too hot nor too cold at any time

temporary, lasting or meant only for a short time; passing soon away; not permanent

ten, one more than nine; half a score

terrify, to make frightened; to fill with terror

theatre, building in which plays are performed

thermometer, (from the Greek *therme,* heat), instrument for measuring temperature

timpani (plural of timpano, from the Latin *tympanum,* that which is beaten), kettledrums

tobacconist, person who sells tobacco

toll, tax or duty paid for use of roads, bridges, etc.

torrent, rushing stream

tourist, person who tours, travelling from place to place

tractable (able to be drawn), easily led or handled, usually applied to persons

tractor (that which draws), vehicle that pulls other vehicles or farm implements

tranquil, calm; peaceful; not agitated. So **tranquillity,** calmness; **tranquillize,** to make calm

trans-, Latin prefix meaning " across ", " beyond ", " on or to the other side "

transmit (*mittere,* to send), to send from one place to another; to pass or hand on; to send over or out

transport (*portare,* to carry), to carry from one place to another; to fill with joy, grief, etc.

triangular, having the shape of a triangle; three-sided

tributary, river serving to swell a larger one

trivial, of little value or importance; trifling

tropical, of the tropics; very hot and wet

truncheon, short wooden club carried by policeman

tubular, having the shape of a tube

tyranny, cruel or despotic use of power; act or behaviour of a tyrant

variegation, fact of being varied in colouring

vegetarian, person who eats only vegetables and fruits

veracity, (from the Latin *verax*, truth), truth; truthfulness

verify, to establish the truth of something. So **verification**

voluntarily, of one's own free will

volunteer, person who enters military or other service of his own free will. So **to volunteer**

voracity, (from the Latin *vorare*, to swallow greedily), greediness in eating; readiness to swallow up or devour

voyager, person who goes on a voyage, travelling by sea or air

warrior, experienced or distinguished soldier

whaler, person who hunts whales; ship he uses

witty, full of wit; amusing; clever

xylophone, (from the Greek *xulon*, wood), musical instrument consisting of strips of wood that vibrate when struck with small wooden hammers